FRONTLINE
A Timeshare Sales Development
Guide

T. A. BRAGG

Frontline © 2019 T. A. Bragg
All rights reserved. No part of this book may be reproduced, stored in a retrieval system, or transmitted in any form or by any means, electronic, mechanical, photocopying, recording, scanning, or otherwise, without the prior written permission of the publisher.

ISBN/SKU: 9781796695878

Growth Publishing L.L.C.
Los Angeles, CA

Project Contributors provided by:
Joshua Edden – Research & Layout Coordinator
Angelica Perry – Manager of Content and Branding @BLVD723
Julian Perry – Visual, Editing and recording@Bigju24
Kimberly Millionaire- Content Editor

DEDICATION

To my lovely wife Camille…
Over 13 years ago two amazing events happened, and in my life hasn't been the same since. First, we thankfully met and ninety days later I began my timeshare career. You have been supportively by my side every step of the way, witnessing all of my successes and my failures. Thank you for being the amazingly wonderful woman you are.
Lovingly, I dedicate this book to you.

T. A.

CONTENTS

DEDICATION	iii
CONTENTS	v
ACKNOWLEDGMENTS	vii
PREFACE	1
INTRODUCTION	6
1. OPPORTUNITY	12
2. NINETY PERCENT	17
3. SEASON & FLOW	22
4. MOTIVATION	39
5. CONFIDENCE	44
6. RELATIONSHIP – THE WARM UP	50
7. QUESTIONS	56
8. VALUE PROPOSITION	65
9. LESS IS MORE	74
10. WHERE ARE YOU?	82
(TEMP CHECK)	82
11. OBJECTIONS	93
12. HOPE & WISH	104
13. HARD WORK & DEDICATION	108
14. URGENCY	112
CONCLUSION	117

ACKNOWLEDGMENTS

First I would like to thank all of the individuals who supported me in my career. Your loyalty has been unwavering and truly sincere. I am truly humbled and I thank you:

Carlton Alexander, Kenny Alexander, Sharifa Al-Ibraheem, Matt Barnes, Guillermo Willy Choren, Chuck Bowman, Steve Coen, Shauna Council, Rita Daniels, Russ Delaney, Kinja Dixon, Monte Duncan, Keenan Frost King, Shonte Gibson, Ann Joseph, Avery Joseph, Neil Karella, Joe Markham, Charles Maurasse, Alex Ovies, Klaleh Parker, Troy Patterson, Aretha Peppers, Shaun Perron, Kain Peta, Brandon Prince, Matt Riggs, Chris Robertson, Jason Sabo, Josh Shohat, Dusty Tonkin, Raul Varela, Michael Washington, Travon Williams and Brandon Willson

IN LOVING MEMORY OF:

Geraldine "Mom" Perry
Jeff Schoor
Kenny and Shelly Adair

PREFACE

The Timeshare Professional is a sales and marketing entity focused on providing substantive development for commissionable representatives in the dynamic timeshare industry. This series focuses on the New Owner, also known as Frontline Sales. As you read this material, you will notice the information is presented differently than the standard corporate training you may have received from your employer. The series will provide an adjusted perspective, diving deeper into the psychology of not just the sales process, but of the inner thoughts, beliefs and understandings of what it takes to be a top performer in the industry of timeshare. The information presented will extend far beyond the basics of what you get from your company's training. It will fill in the gaps, remove any blinders and provide you with insight to what otherwise would be unexpected and unforeseen challenges and perceived impediments to success. You will be able to establish an edifice, a rock solid foundation on which to build a successful timeshare sales career.

Either you've already attended or are about to embark upon your first day of training, a day of excitement, anxiety and the unknown. That first day of training you are told to just show up on Monday morning. You then dive into one to two weeks of training, with the expectation of learning and understanding a new industry, its process, acronyms and jargon, and just simply know what to do.

    I can recall my inception into this business. In the hopes of acclaim and glory into the corporate world, I took this opportunity in my late twenties to jump into something I truly had no inclination of or prior expertise on, selling timeshare. Nonetheless, confidence embedded within me, manifested, and infected every inch of my body as I assessed my peers who not only seemed nervous, but a bit overwhelmed. But that was them; I knew I was in the right place at the right time. The 7:00 AM to 4:00 PM training was an onslaught of sales tactics, materials, ideologies, and terminologies that I had never heard before. It was almost as if I were trying to learn a whole new language in only two weeks.

    After learning the most basic and rudimentary of knowledge about your new career, you're thrust onto the sales floor and thrown to the wolves. When it's your turn to take your first tour and do your first presentation, is when you realize you might not be quite ready. You realize, what was learned in training is not necessarily how the game is actually played. This is one of the biggest challenges new salespeople have to face. They think the process they've learned in training is enough to propel them to the summit of achieving top-level performance, simply because it is provided by the company. They usually do not know that the training is just focused on the rudiments, the fundamentals, the essentials and nothing more.

    The trainers of the timeshare industry are some of the very best of any industry, but they have an extremely difficult task. Timeshare sales in its entirety, is a special, non-formative process that is unique every single tour, and is very challenging to train without over complicating it. I can assure you, you won't achieve the kind of success I know you expect from your new career, if you remain content with just the knowledge you gained from that training. The training is not meant to help a representative completely master the process. However, there are those salespeople that stand out: The Great Ones. These are the people who took their careers in their own hands, seeking knowledge, understanding, growth and mastery of the art and science behind touring a guest who initially wants nothing to do with the product, and in two hours having that same guest ask to own the product. One must think outside the box, consistently learn new tactics, and figure out what triggers deep emotion that creates buying motive and incites buying actions.

In this business you must train on the same level of that of a professional athlete. Those athletes had to be committed to working on their skill set daily to become professionals. Athletes run, lift weights and practice over and over the very basic fundamentals of their game. They're in a constant state of refinement and improvement, to not only become a professional, but to remain a professional. In this business, you must be a salesperson committed to becoming a professional that succeeds at a consistently high level. There's no quick or easy fix nor is there fast money in this business. You might get fortunate or have a "hot streak," but to sustain consistently excellent production, you have to develop your skill set. You have to hone in on the little things that make up the difference between good and great. You have to learn to cross every "T" and dot every "I." You flat out have to go after it. The premonition of "will" comes from within. You have to be a creative thinker, constantly finding that niche that's unrelated to whatever tactic anyone else is using yet confident enough to not be afraid to ask the tough questions.

To succeed in this business you have to be the kind of person who thrives in an environment that's fast-paced, where you constantly have to think on your feet, and be quick-witted. You have to have a very strong desire to win. In timeshare, you compete every single day. Not against your colleagues, but against the guests sitting across from you. The guests want to sell you on why they can't change their lives today, and you're selling them on why they should. You have to whole heartedly believe your guest should make the choice to become a member with you today. Self-confidence and belief are absolute necessary to compete and win. The Mastery is up to you.

The goal of this book is to focus on specific knowledge and insight that one needs to have in order to obtain consistent, high levels of production month over month - Information that you won't get from any other sales book on the market.

Everything you will read in this book is a byproduct of every ethereal notion I learned, used and taught that resulted in my success. All 13 years of that experience have gone into this book. This is just the first of a series of books that cast a net across all commissionable facets of the timeshare industry.

I will delve into all the impeding intangibles of selling timeshare, the mentality needed for consistent success, and the vigorous ambition embedded in this thriving business. This will be your stepping stool, your guide that will innately refine your skills and take them to a new level.

Here is what this book is going to do for you:

It will give you an understanding of many finite nuances of selling timeshare.

It will give you knowledge of situations you will encounter every day on every tour that you weren't necessarily taught to effectively respond to in training.

It will explain the "why" so you can understand the reasons for the action. The "why" is the little nuances that differentiate the good from the great, the sales "reps" from the timeshare professionals. If you really explore and understand the why, the intent of the action taken and reason behind it, the verbiage and delivery of the presentation becomes far more impactful, effective and is internalized. It's the ultimate catalyst in seeing your skills progress astronomically.

Upon reading this book, I ask you to do these following steps to enhance your learning:

- Annotate each chapter
- Highlight key words
- Make note of new ideologies never learned
- Apply notions learned to your practice
- Repeat. Repeat. Repeat.

In order to best absorb the valuable information presented within the pages of this book, have a pen and highlighter ready for use, and eliminate any and all distractions. Once this is achieved, you'll be ready to begin the first chapter.

INTRODUCTION

There are thousands of sales training books out in the market today. Books on real estate sales, car sales, and sales in other niche businesses and industries. Unfortunately, it is rare to see anything that is solely devoted to the timeshare sales industry.

In your training class, you no doubt learned a little history of timeshare and the history of your company. You have definitely learned what your company provides, what sets them apart from their competitors and exactly what makes their product special. Finally, you learned their specific "Steps to the Sale."

The "Steps to the Sale" is the company's road map from hello to congratulations. They are the basic steps of the timeshare sale. You learn your company's steps and then you practice it, piece by piece by piece. Each timeshare company has its own variations of the steps of the sale. They have established a process that is conducive to their product, their site restraints and location, but all include these basic components:

- Meet and Greet
- Intent Statement

- Warm-up
- Discovery
- Presentation
- Explanation/Mechanics
- Resort tour/Kiosk
- Close
- Money

One very important step that precedes any of the basics is pre-sale preparation. This, in my opinion, is the most valuable but most overlooked step one must master to truly become a Timeshare Professional. You must mentally focus and prepare yourself to SUCCEED. Unfortunately, representatives are rarely taught the art of having a "Superior State of Mind" during the two-week training period because of the emphasis on the mechanics of the product.

Yet when you come out of the class, it will be with excitement. You will be eager to start studying, to start learning. Your efforts will be concentrated towards getting better and immediate improvement. One of the things that many people do is to go to a bookstore or go online in search of books on timeshare sales. Over the years, I've found a few books here and there dedicated specifically to timeshare sales. Ultimately, what they have failed to do is look through the owners' perspective, through the eyes of an owner actually experiencing timeshare. Many were written well over a decade ago. Not only are they antiquated, they are basic, rarely expanding above and beyond what is presented in training.

You and I know that one thing is constant, change. The timeshare industry is constantly changing, evolving and growing. What was new and cutting edge when I got in the business in 2006, is no longer new and exciting. Many tactics that worked then, no longer do. Because not only has the industry changed, but so has the consumer. Their needs, wants, desires and understanding of timeshare have changed. In fact, trends and practices that are in vogue now may be extinct in the next five years. The sale isn't the same as it was years ago. This is a much different business today, than it was when most of these books were written.

You may be asking yourself now, in what way has the business changed? I will tell you.

The consumer is much savvier now than he or she was then. The product of timeshare has evolved, which is now vacation ownership, and a points-based system versus a standard week-based system is now fully adapted by the public. When I got into the business in 2006, few people really knew about points. Now the vast majority of consumers know what points are, and don't need to go into great detailed explanations of how they work because it is fully been integrated into the public's consciousness.

The versatility of configuring all aspects of travel has broadened the horizon of timeshare sales to a new set of consumers looking for a less expensive, more effective way of traveling. They're able to use them for airfare, car rentals and hotels. No longer are owners' limitations constricted to only the use of accommodations.

The age of Baby Boomers and Generation X no longer saturate the market due to the rise of Millennials, resulting in a shift in demographics. This generation (born in the era of the internet and technological advance) travels in ways never seen before in past generations. It's caused the industry to change, modify, and adapt to new ventures of travel in order to grasp the new audience's desires.

> "Until you change your thinking, you will always recycle your results."
>
> - T.A. Bragg

The timeshare industry has been around for over fifty years and has spanned over multiple generations. Families have now passed their ownership down multiple times with several generations of families creating memories and enjoying unbelievable experiences together. From this, the industry has become a staple to travel, tradition, and nostalgia to the owners of past, present, and future. In order for this to continue, the industry must keep up with demands by ongoing evolution, enhancements and innovation.

The industry and consumer are going to continue to change and evolve. So you as a sales representative must continuously learn, grow and evolve to keep up and perform consistently high to meet your guests' needs. For example, some millennials don't believe in owning. To some, owning a home, let alone their vacations, is not important. They are happy renting their vacations because it doesn't commit or lock them in. The whole financial logic that this sale this is rooted in, does not apply to them. You have to adapt and evolve your sale to fit them, offering a different financial logic that will appeal to this demographic, like hedging off inflation and freezing the cost of vacations at today's prices forever. Same product, different angle, different approach.

BACK TO BASICS

Top-level performance can only be mastered when you educate yourself on the basics of the timeshare sale process. It becomes imperative that you learn and master the specific basic fundamentals included in this book in order to construct a solid foundation to build a successful career. What I've found is when the foundation is laid correctly you become consistent in this business month in and month out. The problem with most salespeople is they try to master skills that are not on par with where their current skill lies. They focus on closing when they don't know how to open. Rome was not built in a day. You have to stick to the fundamentals until they become second nature and you're able to execute them effortlessly. You must master even the rudimentary and most simple basics like:

- Walking through the door with confidence
- Asking the right questions, at the right time
- Controlling your mindset
- Remembering this is your business

This will bring to light the specifics of the process in the presentation. Unlike the ambiguity of other trainings, we recognize the foundation of how to take our tactics and utilize them when closing the deal. Everything that is taught in this book is used every day on every tour on every frontline sales floor.

THE SECRET

What makes this industry truly special is the fact that you don't have to have some mutant like special physical skill to succeed. For example, if you want to play in the NBA, you traditionally have to have a certain height requirement that's abnormally high above the average height of a regular human being. To play in the NFL, you are going to have to be bigger and faster than the average person. To play baseball you need to have extreme hand-eye coordination than the average person. To be a singer, you are going to have to have a voice that takes people's breath away. These are all God-given abilities that are impossible to obtain naturally.

> "Talent you have naturally. Skill is only developed by hours and hours of beating on your craft."
>
> -Will Smith

In this business, the special talent is simply hard work and dedication. This is indeed the secret sauce that makes every Timeshare Professional consistently succeed. Every person has the opportunity to get to that level of professionalism, talent, and performance. Everyone has that chance to achieve greatness in this business and no matter what site you work at, there's enough pie for everyone. Your success doesn't take away, reduce or minimize any other salespersons success. In this industry, the pie can just get bigger. The secret sauce is you. The perfection of the secret sauce depends on how much of your time, effort, and dedication you to put into getting your piece of the pie.

The consequence of not perfecting the fundamentals leads to a weak foundation. We all know you can't build your castle on a weak foundation, because it will come crumbling down. A weakened foundation will subject you to mediocrity, which can consume your fundamental skill set, and tremendously reduce the level of achievement you're actually capable of. In more ways than one, it will truly be the difference between lasting a few months in this business vs having a long-lasting career and being the individuals that make the money that was promised when entering the business.

1. OPPORTUNITY

"Excuses will always be there for you; Opportunity won't."

- T. A. Bragg

Have you ever had an opportunity to sell a product where once you sold the product, your buyers sincerely thanked you and you were able to congratulate them? How many times have you ever changed a family's life? Literally, with just the unbelievable product you sold them? I'm talking about where a family has an opportunity to do things they thought were impossible. Yet because they simply met you, you made it possible for their only imaginable trips come to life.

For many of you reading this book, this is your first foray into the timeshare industry. Many times timeshare salespeople forget about the tremendous opportunity we have, which is the first thing you will learn on this journey. This opportunity is not just from a spiritual standpoint, but from a financial standpoint as well.

Opportunity is formulated into one equation.

CHALLENGE + CHANGE = OPPORTUNITY.

My sole intent is to resonate this message to all of you readers who should mark this as the first steps into this business. This is fuel that will get you through tough times, challenging tours, and countless other impediments in your way.

It is important for you to own the fact that in this business, there are no limits to what you can earn. You have the opportunity to earn millions of dollars in your career. Thousands of Timeshare Professionals have done it before your time and thousands will continue to do so. Your success all depends on what you do now from this point forward. Not what you've done before, nor what you hope to do in the future, but what you do now.

DIAMONDS IN THE ROUGH

Opportunity is just like a diamond, gold, or iron ore. From the naked eye it seems to be like any other rock grounded in the earth. But once it's extracted, put under immense pressure, and refined to its flawless definition, it formulates into an invaluable object. Opportunity only becomes realized when you reach for it, grab it and capitalize on it. A diamond is just a plain rock until it is mined and refined, an opportunity is just an option until it is taken and executed. How many times have We've all had opportunities placed in front of us and failed to take advantage of them? In 2009, in the mist of the great recession, I had the opportunity to buy my timeshare company's stock for pennies on the dollar. Unfortunately, I never did. if I had wisely taken advantage of that opportunity, I would be millions of dollars richer today because that stock has gone up a thousand-fold.

When an individual has an opportunity placed in front of them like this business offers, the greatest effort and commitment must be given. You should never let it slip through your fingers. You need to commit to seizing this opportunity, and take it incredibly serious so that you can reap the many benefits and financial gains it makes available to you. Otherwise, another will seize that very same diamond and leave you remised.

Offering vacation ownership is a precious opportunity to change the lives of other families and individuals. Timeshares help your guests' marriages, help their children do better in school, strengthen family units and create priceless memories and experiences. When a person leaves this earth, their children and grandchildren won't talk about how much money he or she had; they'll talk about the experiences and memories they made together. These amazing experiences and timeless moments will remain with their family forever. I am an owner of timeshare and after 9 years and 58 trips later, I can completely attest to this fact. Changing the lives of so many other people gives us the mandate to reap the self-satisfaction and financial reward provided by this industry. Simply put, we become able to provide a greater quality of life for our families because we so positively affect many other families. The reality is, there are very few six-figure jobs knocking on the door. If there were, you'd probably have one already. You are here, selling timeshares because you see the big picture, you believe in what you do, and you have a desire for succeeding so much so that you are willing to work for it and will it to fruition.

> "Success happens when preparation meets opportunity."
>
> -Unknown

Timeshare is often used as gifts to loved ones. For instance, parents may share it with their newly married children to go and enjoy their honeymoon. People often offer their timeshare to their friends who can't afford to otherwise go away and have the vacation of a lifetime. It's amazing, what we do and what we sell; we bring countless joy to numerous people.

I know some have doubts about this opportunity called timeshare. You may be asking yourself if this is for you or if you are cut out for this business. That is a profound question so you may want to ponder this; what does your gut tell you? Is changing people's lives important to you? Does selling a product that will enhance somebody's personal well-being and is that purposeful to you? Are you willing to give everything you have in your proverbial gas tank to change someone's life? How good are you at overcoming challenges or dealing with change?

SEIZE THE OPPORTUNITY

Lawyers go to school for 6 years, doctors go to school for 8 years. Both careers can potentially earn incomes in the $200,000 and up range simply because of the impact they have on individuals lives. They are smart individuals who have significantly worked the hardest and were dedicated to mastering their craft. We, in the timeshare industry have that same opportunity to impact individual lives and earn that type of income year after year after year. It is imperative for Salespeople to treat this opportunity in the same regard as the law student or the medical student treated their preparation into those lucrative professions. You must treat this like the quarter million dollar a year job it is.

In this business you will encounter tumultuous challenges that will try to hinder that self-confidence. Throughout the succession of my career, I've had the experience of training, working, and observing countless of individuals with enormous amounts of opportunity amassed in front of them that was not seized. They cast their precious diamonds back into the ground from which they came simply because they could not see the incredible treasure of the opportunity before them. if you lack in self-confidence then you must emphatically strengthen it for if you don't, you too will never seize those very same opportunities.

The financial reward is too tremendous to give anything less than 100% of your efforts into this career. Remember that we are selling fun and excitement. We are truly giving our guests the opportunity to see the world, live life, and create a tradition for the next generations to continue and repeat. This is what makes this profession so special and unique.

CHAPTER SUMMARY - OPPORTUNITY

- Opportunity only becomes realized when you reach for it and grab it

- It is important for you to own the fact that in this business, there are no limits to what you can make.

- You must be creative, constantly finding that niche that's unrelated to whatever tactic anyone else is doing yet confident enough to ask the tough questions.

- Your presentation should be all about helping your guests, not about you.

- Guests want to sell you on why they can't change their lives today, and you're selling them why they should.

2. NINETY PERCENT

"It all begins and ends in your mind. What you give power to, has power over you, if you allow it."
- Unknown

Many times, a salesperson entering this industry is looking for that one line that will make them great. I'm here to tell you there's no one line or special "pitch" that will accomplish that. But there's one thing that outweighs every other and that's the salesperson's mentality.

90% of a salesperson's success derives from his or her mentality, mindset and will. Will, in its essence is, your emotional state of mind, your conviction, passion, your perception, your role, and most importantly, your focus. In my tenure, I've seen individuals go from rags to riches and vice versa simply because of their mentality. It's what a particular Timeshare Professional coined "A superior state of mind". The Timeshare Professional has a superior state of mind from the moment they open their eyes to the second they close them.

The expectation of success is the embodiment of the Superior State of Mind. It's that infallible term "winner win." That attitude, that appreciation, incepts a belief and confidence in the product and themselves. These categorical individuals always look for the way IN and never the way OUT. They are true problem solvers, not problem encouragers. The realization of the only constant in this business is change which makes them comfortable with their "cheese being moved." They understand the infinite mountain of no's that proceed them, yet seek the opportunity to change every no into a yes. They remain in equilibrium, unparsed by the ups and downs that the emotional rollercoaster of a business brings to them. Effort should be challenged by no one and ambition is always at 100%. A professional's diction coheres their mentality. They say, "I want to go to training." Instead of "I have to go to training."

> "If you want to win big. You've got to stop thinking small."
>
> - Unknown

Timeshare is more than a business, Timeshare is your business and your personal branding of how you sell and what you sell. The money profited from this industry is simply too bountiful to not take advantage of the opportunity that is ubiquitous. It's treating this opportunity as your business that makes the good transform to great. A business owner analyzes their strengths and weaknesses, they create targets in which they must perform, and they reconcile with what they must do day after day to ensure success is consistent. Emulate your 90% into that of an owner of a successful business. Treat this as your own personal multi-million dollar business and you will see how your performance increases exponentially. In my tenure, I've seen individuals go from rags to riches and vice versa simply because of their mentality. Again, 90% of a salesperson's success is tied into their mentality and mind set.

THE HAVES

A superior state of mind is oddly enough a trait that 90% of timeshare salespeople do not walk thru the door with. The 10% that possess it, always have the leg up on everyone else. Key indications of a superior state of mind are as follows:

I. The Representative is confident enough to take any and all tours handed to them without hindrance of ability
II. The Representative's mood is tenacious, jubilant, and unaffected by misery and all the company that infects it
III. The Representative is well dressed; always dressed to impress rather than appearing depressed.
IV. The Representative is fearless, constantly tries to close the deal without worry of objection or "push back"
V. The Representative is ambitious yet humble, recognizing their level of skill in their craft, yet always seeking to sharpen their ability whilst helping others.

Once these indications become applicable to you, the possibilities are absolutely endless.

THE HOW

Reaching a superior state of mind involves a constant "put together" for oneself. THE WAY IN is more than a three-word euphemism for finding the deal. It's seeing any situation and figuring out the best approach needed to win. Finding a way in is creating the deal with those challenging tours that are inevitable.

Initially your self-assurance is going to be imbalanced, so teetered, that you feel unsure and like a fish out of water. I am here to tell you that this is a normal feeling for every great salesperson when they began in this industry. I've seen many salespeople start their careers with an endless downward spiral, constantly worrying about why they are failing. It wasn't until they put in the work to find their niche that made their 90% fuel them to the highest performance. Superior state of mind lies in your 90%.

> "Watch your thoughts, for they become words. Watch your words, for they become actions. Watch your actions, for they become habits. Watch your habits, for they become your skill set. Work on your skill set, for they are the keys to your success."-
> T.A. Bragg

THE HAVE NOTS

A superior state of mind is so essential that not achieving it will only limit your potential. You will become susceptible to folding into yourself. The industry becomes an unwelcoming place to walk into day after day. Suddenly, the place with ubiquitous opportunity becomes daunting. The below pattern procures if your superior state of mind becomes weak:

I. You forget to take responsibility of your own actions, causing you cast blame on management, the company, or your peers
II. Your confidence lessens every day you walk in.
III. The fire that was once ablaze has now died down to a small flicker.

Those who fall in this three-step pattern often find it hard to dig themselves out. In this industry, only the ones who become so well adapt survive. They've got to maintain that superior state of mind. As you grow in this business, surround yourself with individuals that possess a mindset of success.

> Surround yourself with individuals that possess a mindset of success.

The 90% of sales people that don't act in a manner of a Timeshare Professional should not be encompassed in your circle.

You attract what you act, especially in this type of atmosphere. Often, you see probability coming into play from the product of your environment. A person who hangs around driven and successful people develops a proneness to be driven and a culture of success. That's why Fortune 500 companies stress their culture from their inception, so they don't lose their 90%. In result, they only hire people who are melded in with the culture so that their values do not cease to exist. Identify yourself in the category of "THE HAVES" instead of implementing yourself with "THE HAVE NOTS." Otherwise, failure will be nonetheless impending regardless of your best efforts.

CHAPTER SUMMARY – NINETY PERCENT

- 90% of a salesperson's success derives from his mentality, mindset and will.

- The expectation of success is the embodiment of the "Superior State of Mind."

- Timeshare is more than a business, it's your business.

- Treat this business as your business and you will see how your performance increases exponentially.

- A superior state of mind is so essential that not possessing it will only limit your potential in this industry.

3. SEASON & FLOW

"A tour is like a river. You can't touch the same water twice, because the flow that has passed will never pass again. There're no "Be Backs" in timeshare; this is a today business."

- T. A. Bragg

A typical month of sales reminds me of two specific things, Seasons and a River. The makeup of these two occurrences greatly affects the matter in which you approach the sale. You can enhance your approach by observing from this perspective.

SEASONS

When I see a sales month, I see 3 different seasons:
- The 1st through the tenth
- The 11th through the 20th
- The 21st through the end of the month.

The 1st 10 days	(1st – 10th)
The 2nd 10 days	(11th – 20th)
The 3rd 10 days	(21st – 30th/31st)

I have always advised sales people to break their month into three parts. I like to use the old saying, "what's the best way to eat an elephant? One bite at a time." When a salesperson gives himself or herself a shorter duration to track and focus on, the month becomes more efficiently manageable to hit the short-term target. A sales month, just like an entire calendar year, is a long time and various obstacles can transpire. Any one particular year can be filled with many good days or many bad ones. A particular year can start off great and end up challenging. Sometimes, nothing eventful happens but this is very rare. Life has an interesting way of giving a person a little of everything. How you deal with those inevitable good times and challenges usually determines how happy you are. If the constant volatility of life proves to be challenging for you, then unhappiness permeates. Happiness is life's currency.

Such is the case with a typical timeshare sales month. There are good days and there are challenging ones, and like we just discussed in the previous chapter, you have to be mentally strong enough to weather the storms. Breaking a sales month into 10-day increments helps the salesperson have several small wins or loses so to never get too high or too low. They don't get lost in the seas of change, they merely stay the course. No matter how harsh a winter or hot a summer, we enjoy the beauty of both, endure the worst of its days, and are always optimistic knowing that seasons change. Your tours are the same way, so embrace, endure and enjoy its seasons.

RIVER

Another remarkable characteristic of a timeshare month is what I call "flow." Just as the flow of a river is predictable, tours assigned to a salesperson within the month are also predictable. I prefer to break a salesperson's body of tours for the month into smaller 10 tour increments. Every 10 tours have a group of IDEAL guests, WORKABLE guests, and guests that UNDER NO CIRCUMSTANCE will allow themselves to be open minded enough to see any value or allow anything to resonate. There's simply NO SHOT (or chance) to create a sell. When this ebb and flow is understood and accepted by the salesperson, three things are realized.

> "Greatness is a bunch of small things done well. Month after month, week after week, day after day, tour after tour. Consistency is the key."
>
> - T. A. Bragg

I. This is a numbers game.
II. The more hands you shake, the more money you make.
III. Identifying and knowing which category your guests fall in allows you to work smarter, not harder.

Categorization allows for the salesperson to either hold themselves accountable for missing their deal or take the pressure off when there was no sale to be had anyway. Reflect back to the saying, "pressure bursts pipes." I've seen reps create self-inflicting pressure that has dismantled their careers. It's important to never put unwarranted pressure on yourself.

These particular insights, a month's 3 different seasons and the months flow of tours will help you better strategize, assess, attack, overcome and exceed your goals every month. It becomes your road map to executing your targets and winning the month. Without a map, signs or landmarks to help guide them how can anyone find their destination?

A MONTH OF 3 SEASONS

As salespeople, one of the first habits taught to us is to set our goals or sales targets; so every month we do just that. We set these goals early, when there's only the unknown. We don't know what will happen, what guest we may get, what challenges we will face, what impediments we'll run into, and how the circumstances may change. As these conditional elements reveal themselves, adjustments need to take place. We have to adjust our strategy, adjust our targets, reassess and reexamine what we need to do to ultimately win at the end of the month. This is extremely challenging when the month is lumped together and looked at as one single body of time. Make your month and goals manageable by breaking it up into 3 distinct periods. Each period is also distinctly different in your guests' thought process along with your own. Each period has its own set of challenges and urgencies. Let's take a closer look:

Commission Breath
The odorous smell of desperation and angst

1st-10th

- A salesperson is either excited about the previous month's results or not. Sometimes the challenge of coming off a great previous month is a lowered motivation in the next month. Sometimes a challenging previous month can deflate the salesperson's confidence for the next month. Let's avoid both possibilities. It never matters what you did last month, it only matters what you're going to do this month.
- Every other salesperson is at ZERO. Everyone has the opportunity to be number 1. When a salesperson starts the month FAST (Multiple deals), he or she greatly increases the odds of having a very successful month.
- The false narrative of "there's a lot of month left" can be an extremely lethal thought process for a salesperson to have. You've let yourself off the hook for the lack of results and aren't holding yourself accountable for those results, enabling a lack of urgency that lent to the existing result.

- Guest usually come in a little less willing to relinquish their money. In their minds, there are still bills to be paid for the month.

11th-20th

- I found over my career that 120%-130% more business is written in the latter part of the month than in the first. Partly because salespeople have greater urgency built up because half the month is over, but also our guest have paid most, if not all of their household bills. Our guests are more financially receptive to spending money, which makes them naturally more open minded and susceptible to the possibility of buying our product.
- The second season is pivotal in regards to how your month will probably end. Your performance during this season most times will either MAKE or BREAK your month. A salesperson's full and complete focus is encouraged during this season.
- Complacency. Many sales people become lulled in the second season of the month. They started off excited, but dealt with some challenges and obstacles that dulled their enthusiasm and lessened their urgency level.
- Distractions. Sometimes, things happen in life or at work early on in the month that diverts one's attention from the task at hand.

21st to END OF MONTH

- Guest are traditionally, as a whole, more open-minded and receptive to our products value proposition, features, benefits and cost due to their financial obligations have been met for the month.
- Panic now begins to set in with salespeople that are performing poorly. This often results in overselling or "commission breath." Greed rears its head for the salespeople over performing during this part of the month, keep in mind Gordon Gecko's statement from the movie Wall Street: "Greed is good." Sometimes

complacency can also overcome an over performing sales person during this time as well.
- Due to higher levels of effort and energy, sometimes "steps" are skipped or missed.
- An attitude of desperation can kick in which results in a less confident sales presentation and a fear to close.

With a greater understanding of the different seasons along with the incremental digestion of the month, now the goals you place across the month can be more manageable and achievable and you as the salesperson can devise the necessary tactics and strategies to win each small battle.

GOAL SETTING USING 3 SEASONS METHOD

Goal setting has always come easy to me. Whatever top-level bonus is, that's my goal. But over the years I've learned there is so much more to goal setting than just picking a arbitrary number. You have to...

- Pick a specific and realistic goal – one that you have come close to but have not hit before.
- Add rescissions to your volume target.
- Break the goal down by the monthly season.

Pick a specific and realistic goal

As I just mentioned, I always set my target parameters around what my top-level bonus was. But this is indicative to my personality make up. I'm an all-in or all out, go big or go home type of individual. Many people are more measured. So when determining a set target, identify a few things first.

Do you feel you can actually hit your target?

- If you have 3 days on the sales floor and you've never even sold one deal, let's not make your target 20 deals for the month.

Have you ever come close to reaching your suggested target?

- If you've never hit any bonus level before, let's not make top-level bonus next month's goal.

Has anyone else ever achieved or exceeded that target?

If the very best salesperson on your sales floor has never written $1 million in volume, there's a great chance that you won't next month.

Pick a target you have come close to but have not hit before.

- I encourage salespeople to push themselves, but don't overexert themselves. If you push yourself in the gym, you will see results. If you overexert yourself in the gym, there's a good chance you're going to hurt yourself. Set your goals modestly above your best performing month. Always set your intentions higher than your past achievements. This applies a stronger nudge on you to keep climbing. The goal is to get to the apex. Just like climbing Mt. Everest, climbing to top-level bonus requires many of the same mentality traits. The difference however is, once we reach top-level, we never want to come back down.

All good salespeople prepare goals at the start of every month, but the great sales people go one step further. The best salespeople in the timeshare industry understand rescissions or cancellations are a part of our business and sales process. The only time there are zero rescissions are when there are zero sales being made. So with that being said, rescissions have to be added or "baked" into your specific targets. This is called a "Rescission Adjustment". Rescission adjustments account for the probable percentage of canceled volume you will encounter. The frontline rescission adjustment is normally 20%. This means, when making your volume targets every month, add an additional 20% of volume to your target.

Example: Target = $100,000 vol

   Res. Adj = 20%

   Adjusted Target: $100,000 X 120% = $120,000

A target of $100,000 becomes an adjusted target of $120,000 once a rescission adjustment of 20% is factored in. This method allows for the salesperson to strategize and create a plan to work toward the correct target number. It also allows for greater performance consistency and continuous success in reaching his or her goals. It's never fun to continuously fall short of one's goals.

Most timeshare sales reps don't realize the companies they work for established their targets in this same fashion. As a timeshare professional, always look for the smartest and most efficient ways to succeed.

MAPPING YOUR GOALS

Now that a goal has been set, it's time to map out your goals over the course of a calendar month. There are on average 22 working days in every calendar month other than the month of February. If you spread those 22 working days across the 3 seasons of the month, you will have 7 working days per season with an extra day in one of the seasons. To map your month, you want to know how much volume you need to produce per season or every calendar 10 days.

Looking at this example, the salesperson would need only $38,200 in volume every 7 working days.

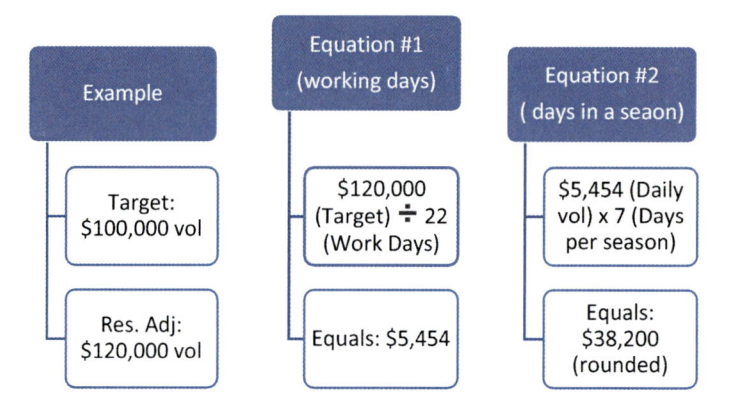

Example	Equation #1 (working days)	Equation #2 (days in a season)
Target: $100,000 vol	$120,000 (Target) ÷ 22 (Work Days)	$5,454 (Daily vol) x 7 (Days per season)
Res. Adj: $120,000 vol	Equals: $5,454	Equals: $38,200 (rounded)

There is a positive psychological effect in breaking your numbers down to much more manageable targets. $38,200 at face value looks much more achievable than $120,000. Even after several challenging days, $38,200 doesn't seem to be out of reach. However, after several challenging days, $120,000 in volume seems even further away and more difficult to achieve.

From an analytical perspective this method is also important. It allows the salesperson to identify he or she is falling behind sooner in the month, rather than later once the month has gotten away from them. When chasing a month-long target, a salesperson will hold on to the hope that things will turn around before taking actions to turn it around himself.

By mapping three different seasons, the salesperson achieves three smaller and easier wins than just one big win. This goes back to the old saying, "What's the best way to eat an elephant? One bite at a time."

CHASE DEALS NOT VOLUME

I've been a part of the timeshare industry for 13 years, and for that entire time, goals and targets have always been based on volume. In 2010, while trying to figure out how to do even better in driving business I came up with a crazy concept. I said, "Let's not drive volume, let's convert that volume into the number of deals needed to hit that volume and that number will psychologically appear much easier to achieve."

Example
- Res. Adj. Target Volume per Season: $38,200
- APT (Average Per Transaction): $19,000

Equation
$$\$38,200 / \$19,000$$

Solution
- 2.01 or 2 deals every season

What I found when converting the target volume to number of deals is the confidence of the salespeople increased exponentially because from a general perspective 2 deals in 10 calendar days seems completely achievable. Their minds were able to easily digest the thought of writing 2 deals in 10 days. $38,200 is easier to conceive than $120,000, we just kept it simple. Remember the acronym, KISS.

I also don't believe in chasing volume because the size of the deal you write is out of your control. Salespeople cannot control their guests' pocketbooks, travel habits, time off of work or any other thing that has to do with their guests' personal lives. The job of the salesperson is one thing and one thing only; Make Them Want It! Make enough of your 20-30 guest want your product and enough of them will purchase, resulting in consistent, high-level production for you. Just focus on making them Want It.

FLOW

There's an expression in this industry that I absolutely love: The Timeshare business isn't a hope and wish. The statement is expressing that success doesn't come from the salesperson hoping or wishing for a deal or for a "good tour." Success in timeshare is manifested. Deals are created, then taken. No guest jumps across the table, grabs the pen out of the salesperson's hand and says, "Where do I sign up at?" Nobody walks through the door ready to buy timeshare that day. The fact is, every single guest that walks through the front door is on tour for the gift.

Even though all sales are created and no one comes in to purchase timeshare, some guest are actually more apt to see value in timeshare than others, while some, under no circumstances will allow themselves to be opened minded enough to even consider timeshare.

In early 2009, I wanted to really get a sense of the shared characteristics of a typical timeshare buyer. What I found was there are 4 specific characteristics new members/owners have in common. As I wrapped my head around this discovery, I

---

9 Winning Moves for Timeshare Success:

Commit to your goals.

Challenge yourself to achieve something you never thought possible.

Seek out coaches and mentors in the industry.

Use challenging tours to advance your learning,

Don't compromise your goals for naysayers fears influence.

Eliminate excuses.

Stay laser focused on your desired result.

Execute on your purpose, despite your fears.

Find an industry specific, skilled circle of influence.

- T.A. Bragg

used an analogy to fully grasp this realization. It goes; when you make a cake and it tastes good, you have to follow the steps perfectly and you have to use precise ingredients. If your ingredients are all correct but you don't use the correct measurements, you can still make the cake, but it won't taste as good. If you don't use all the ingredients, you won't have a cake at all. I began calling those characteristics, the ingredients. These 4 ingredients, if possessed by the guest, should be a deal 70%-100% of the time. Once I identified those common characteristics, I then searched for the characteristics in guests that did not purchase. This became extremely valuable information and insight, because I began seeing their "why nots." If a salesperson knows what the reasons the guest's give for not purchasing he's able to attack the objection early in the presentation. I then wanted to gauge how many guests with all four characteristics came in on tour, on average every 10 tours and how many were missing one or more of the characteristics. I began to recognize patterns in the flow of tours of the salespeople on my team. So, I began quantifying my observations and putting the results on paper. What I discovered was pretty consistent results that represent the typical flow of tours: I assigned each tour type a category, A, B or C.

> You are not trying to convince them your guest of anything. You're trying to show them how you are going to make their lives better.
>
> -Marc Cuban
> (adapted)

Category A

- Have all 4 ingredients.
- You CAN NOT miss these deals. These deals are the foundation of the salesperson's performance. Executing on these tours allows a salesperson to "make a living" selling timeshare.

Category B

- Missing 1-2 ingredients.

- Can still be sold. Obviously, there challenges to getting a deal, but not impossible. The very best in the industry find a way to sell some of these tours and overcome the challenges.

Category C

- Missing 3 to all of the ingredients.
- The chances of converting these tours are slim to none, but the very best, work smarter not harder. If the salesperson is not going to get any financial gain from this guest type, the best get some type of value out of the tour by working on a specific part of their presentation that needs improving or tweaking, or just trying something new they've come up with. Get better on these tours, by working on a new strategy or technique with no fear of possibly "losing the deal". You have nothing to lose and everything to gain.

Breakdown

Total Tours: 10

- Category A= 3 out of 10 tours or 30% of tours
    - A salesperson must sell 2-3 of this tour type.
- Category B= 4 out of 10 tours or 40% of tours
    - A salesperson must sell 1-2 of this tour type.
- Category C= 3 out of 10 tours or 30% of tours
    - A salesperson must get better on all 3 of this tour type.

Category Breakdown

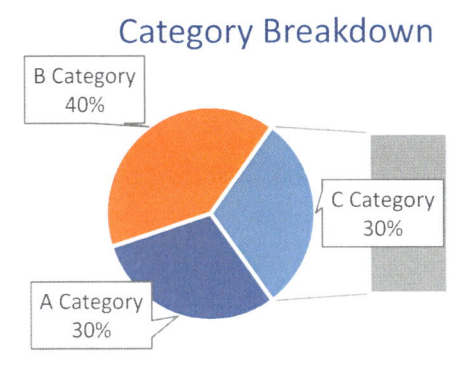

- B Category 40%
- A Category 30%
- C Category 30%

When broken down, the numbers are eye opening.

* A salesperson has a shot at getting a deal with 70% of the guests they tour.

A salesperson has a "Very good" shot at getting a deal with 43% of the 70% of guest they tour and have a shot at.

Understanding this information allows a salesperson to do several things:

I. Work Smarter not Harder - A salesperson can now identify earlier which ingredients are missing, identify the inevitable objection and overcome it early.

II. Perform more efficiently - A salesperson can identify if their guest has all the ingredients early, which allows for them to do every single thing in their power not to miss the sale. If a salesperson executes on the A category tours, they'll never perform below minimum sales standards.

III. Take the pressure off themselves - When a salesperson can identify the guest that are least receptive to their product early in the presentation, they can take the pressure off themselves and transition to getting some type of value out of that tour sooner.

THE KEY

The Key to unlocking consistent, high level results is to get 7 out of 10 of your tours interested. Get those guests to strongly consider buying your product and asking you and the T.O. for a few minutes to talk privately. If 70% of your tours have genuine interest, I can guarantee 2-4 of those guests are going to say yes.

Know where your shots are and know where they are not. If you are laser focused, determined and unequivocal in your pursuit of the deal on 70% of your total tours, and smart enough to recognize early the 30% you're going to get better on, I can promise you 4 things...

1. You're going to sell more

2. You're going to be more consistent

3. You're going to be less stressed and happier

4. You and your presentation are going to get better every month

Remember, The Flow Doesn't Change!

THE GRAND FINALE: THE INGREDIENTS

1. Travel/Vacation Commitment

2. Can afford at least $300 per month in payment

3. Has good enough credit to be approved for the various down payment assistance apparatuses or can put down a minimum of $2,000 today

4. Must be decent human beings

In the timeshare industry, we sell travel, vacations and dreams. If guests don't do or have at least 1 of the 3, it's going to be tough selling them a lifetime of travel, vacations and dreams. If the guest truly can't afford the salesperson's smallest package, then the salesperson can't sell them a package. If the guest has challenged credit or no discretionary savings means they are unable to make a down payment, a salesperson can't sell them. Remember, your job is to sell the product and make your guest want it. You as the salesperson cannot do anything about their financial abilities or the guest credit worthiness. Control what you can control.

Lastly, if a guest is simply put, a disgusting human being the product traditionally will not resonate with them. Good people see a value in "getting away and spending quality time with their loved ones." Not so good people usually don't.

There's no magic to this, just good ol' common sense, tethered to a mentality of seeking the way in and never the way out. Though there is no magic to this, there is a science to it. Reread this chapter and really absorb the information. Conquer the seasons of the month and master the flows, it's a game changer.

CHAPTER SUMMARY – SEASONS & FLOW

- When a salesperson gives themselves a shorter duration to track and focus on, it becomes more manageable and efficient to hit the short-term target.

- There is a positive psychological effect in breaking your numbers down to much more manageable targets.

- Categorization allows for the salesperson to either hold themselves accountable for missing their deal or take the pressure off of them when there was no deal to be had anyway.

- We must adjust our strategy, adjust our targets, reassess and reexamine what we need to do to ultimately win at the end of the month.

- If a salesperson knows what the no's will be, they're able to attack the objection early in the presentation.

- Know where your shots are and know where they are not.

4. MOTIVATION

"Motivation is what gets you started. Habit is what keeps you going."

- Jim Rohn

The timeshare industry is what I call a "performance-based business." Meaning, you're only as good as your previous month's sales performance. A salesperson's existence on any timeshare sales floor is results driven; meaning, goals and targets are extremely important. But goals are set every month and many times, by most salespeople, those goals each month are missed or not met. I believe there's a specific reason for this. As a timeshare sales person, you never have control of the tours you're handed, who the people are or what's going on in their lives; but every timeshare salesperson has total and complete control of, his or her individual efforts.

You, as the salesperson determine whether you give 100% effort or less than 100% effort. I get it. There are days when you simply woke up on the wrong side of the bed, you partied too much the previous night, you're tired, you're a little under the weather, you've stubbed your toe getting ready for work, you had an argument with your spouse or your kids, you've had a string of tough tours and a million other reasons why you're not at your best. Unfortunately, when these personal issues upset a salesperson guess what there's less of? Effort! On those days when there's less effort, the odds of missing a deal greatly increase. A missed deal here, a missed deal there and Voilà goals are missed. I always encouraged my team to leave any personal issues at the front door. Your workplace should be deemed a sanctuary for you to leave all worries behind and excel. On your sales floor, you are no longer a parent with three kids dealing with the challenges of parenthood. You're no longer a mid-twenties college student repaying college loans. You're no longer the post retired adult looking for extra cash that goes beyond social security pay checks. Here you are a **Timeshare Professional** who is committed to both financial and workplace excellence. That can only be achieved through the highest potential of effort.

THE DOMINO EFFECT

The truth is, most salespeople don't even realize their giving less effort. They go through their process normally, following all the steps to the tee, but maybe at the end they don't try to overcome that fifth or sixth "no." See, less effort is not a lack of effort. Less effort is subtle, but big enough to lose a deal. When a salesperson misses a deal, chances are he or she is going to miss their goals. It's the cumulative effect that inevitably takes a toll on a sales representative. A missed opportunity creates a missed deal, a missed deal becomes a missed goal, a missed goal generates less productivity, less productivity will generate ultimately into less opportunity. This domino effect can eventually come to a head and completely demoralize the salesperson from ever reaching success again.

> You will never always be motivated. You have to learn how to be disciplined.
> - Unknown

THE WHY

As a sales leader, I needed to keep my team's efforts high which increased my chances of hitting my goals. If I could increase their efforts daily, and keep them consistently high, more of the salespeople on my team would hit their goals and subsequently so would I. The first step I took was to look at myself. For my entire career, I've prided myself on always giving 100% effort, and I asked myself why? That question led me to identifying my internal motivation and realizing how it drove my efforts to accomplish my goals. What I found was goals are nothing but numbers on a piece of paper until you put forth the effort to achieve them, but effort can fluctuate and even wane if you don't have something driving that effort. Motivation. Your internal motivation will push you when you're tired, sick, or upset and refocus you when you've lost focus. Motivation is like sugar. Sugar is sweet no matter what the weather is like, how you feel, what you're thinking or anything happening around you. No matter what, sugar is going to still be sweet. What lights a fire deep inside of you, that motivation, is lit no matter how you feel, what's happening in your life or around you.

Since entering this industry, have you done any soul searching? Have you looked deep down into yourself and found what lights your fire? If not, what are you waiting for? The treasures and rewards in this industry are too big to not dig deep and figure out the answer to this question. When you identify your motivation, you also unlock another answer to a very important question. Why do you want to hit your goals?

When is the last time you asked yourself, "Why do I want to hit my goals?" When we know the what's and whys, we have a true understanding of our actions and that understanding gives your actions purpose. . The funny thing is, the answer to what is your motivation and why you want to hit your goals, should be the same answer.

So, what's your motivation? Figure it out. Is your motivation to be the very best at your site or in your company? Is your motivation to make a lot of money? Is your motivation your family, providing for them and giving them the very best out of life? Whatever your motivation is, seek it out, find it, identify it and then own it. Write it down and give it life. When you write it down, you make it real; and it becomes tangible.

THE MONEY MOTIVATION

If your motivation is solely financial, "it's all about the Benjamins," I get it. You have a tremendous opportunity to make a lot of money in this business. What I've tried to do over the years is go deeper and think bigger than just money. I've met hundreds of salespeople with money as their main motivation and a great number of them experienced months where their motivations drove them to making large amounts of money. Their motivation was money, which meant there why was money. They made the money; now what? They've reached their personal pinnacle and got to the mountaintop. Now what? Where else do they climb to? What motivation do they have left? When you reach your why, the what now has less power. Look at many championship boxers or mixed martial arts fighters. Their motivation was to win a title. After winning that title, most are never the same fighter again. They lose their hunger and drive. Your motivation must be greater than money. Your motivation must be something that will drive you for the entire year, maybe your career or even your lifetime. To give your motivation sustainability, it must be greater than you.

This isn't just about goals, it's about the motivation to reach those goals. What the salesperson must do is change their perspective. Adjust and recalibrate your perspective to increase the odds of hitting what you're shooting for, accomplishing what you want and achieving greater results. It's simply not enough, to just have a goal.

CHAPTER SUMMARY - MOTIVATION

- You're only as good as your previous month's sales performance.

- On those days when there's less effort, the odds of missing a deal greatly increase.

- A missed opportunity creates a missed deal, a missed deal becomes a missed goal, a missed goal generates less productivity, less productivity will generate ultimately into less opportunity.

- What lights a fire deep inside of you, that motivation - lit no matter how you feel, what's happening in your life or around you?

- Your motivation must be something that will drive you for the entire year, maybe your career or even your lifetime.

5. CONFIDENCE

"Self-confidence is infectious to your guest. How can anyone see how great you are if you can't see it yourself."

- T. A. Bragg

The overall perception of timeshare sales or sales in general is there are ups and downs. The belief is, one month is good and the next is bad. For salespeople who choose to treat their occupation as a job, yes, those salespeople will experience volatility in their sales results. But there are a group of salespeople that treat their occupation as a career and commit themselves to becoming professionals in their sales field. In the timeshare industry there is a vast difference between a timeshare representative and a Timeshare Professional and it's just not in the net result of their performance or pay check. A great part of the difference is the professional's confidence, confidence in themselves, in their skill set, in their product, in their company and in their industry.

CONFIDED CONFIDENCE

What's interesting about confidence is it can't be taught; either you have it, or you don't. Though you can't teach confidence, one can gain confidence. Confidence gained is unique. You're not born with it; someone else didn't instill it in you; you didn't learn it from a book, and you don't catch it like a cold. What makes confidence gained so unique is that it's rooted in something that's infallible and can never be taken from you. Confidence is rooted in study, training, development, understanding, repetition, commitment, dedication and hard work. It establishes a belief system in yourself and in your inevitable success. When a salesperson commits themselves to internalizing their steps, their processes, their product, their company, their competitors and to the art of selling, only then have they taken control of their careers. Being in control of one's life breeds confidence.

> The greatest
> "I figured that if I said it enough, I would convince the world that I really was the greatest."
>
> -Cassius Clay

Confidence: you can't see it and you can't touch, but amazingly you know when you're in the presence of it. I'm not talking about cockiness or arrogance, but complete belief in one's self. All timeshare professionals have it and use it as a tool to ensure their success. Their confidence doesn't turn off and on, there's no switch. From the second they wake up to get ready for work, until they walk out of their sales site, they're exuding confidence.

A typical timeshare professional's workday:

I. Wake up feeling great and believing they're going to get a deal today
II. Getting ready for work and excited because they believe they're going to get a deal today

III. Commuting to work, eager to get there believing their deal is on the way to the sales site to meet them
IV. Walks into sales site beaming because they believe they're about to meet the guests who will be their deal
V. Enthusiastically goes to greet their first guests of the day that they believe are their deal
VI. Passionately, they present their product to their guests believing they're a deal
VII. Confidently, they ask their guests to buy their product from them today because they've earned the right to and believe they're sitting across from their deal
VIII. Respectfully and honestly, they overcome all objections because they feel their guests need their product and believe they're a deal
IX. Without hesitation, extends their hand and congratulates their guests for becoming their newest owner/member

Is the Timeshare Professional day a little different than a timeshare representative?

A typical timeshare "rep's" workday:
I. Wakes up hoping they get a tour today
II. Gets ready for work hoping that if they get a tour, it's a good tour
III. Commutes to work wishing their guests from yesterday said yes
IV. Lethargically walks into their sales site, unsure if they'll even get a tour
V. Commiserates with other timeshare representatives who are also unsure if they'll even get a tour
VI. Waits and wishes to get a tour
VII. Receives a tour and nervously goes to meet their guest

VIII. Clumsily teaches their guest about the company and product
IX. "Kind of" asks their guest to buy from them
X. Half-heartedly attempts to overcome their guest's objections
XI. Completely understanding of their guest's decision to not buy from them today, but hopeful to see them when they come back in a couple of years and sneaks the guest their number

Do you notice a difference between the work day of a Timeshare Professional and the work day of a timeshare representative? I know your workday is not like this, but do you know any salespeople whose day probably looks just like this?

A timeshare professional's confidence comes from their commitment of time, a laser focus on learning, dedication to understanding and the hard work of fine tuning. They wake up knowing they have opportunity, a superior state of mind and an internal motivation that wills them to success. The confidence gained, exudes from them the second they open their eyes until the second they say good night.

TRANSFER OF ENTHUISIASM

The timeshare sale is a transfer of energy, enthusiasm and emotion from the salesperson to the guest. That first transfer happens the moment you call out your guests' names in the lobby and extend your hand for a formal introduction. It's rare to lose a deal in the introduction, but a salesperson can significantly reduce their chances at a deal with a lack of confidence during introductions.

If a timeshare salesperson is not confident and enthusiastic about their product, how will their guest be confident enough in the product to spend $30,000 in two hours? The confidence a Timeshare Professional emits, gives the guest more confidence in them, their product, their company and most importantly in the guests' buying choice that day. Confidence and the creation of a sale go hand in hand.

CHAPTER SUMMARY - CONFIDENCE

- In the timeshare industry there is a vast difference between a timeshare representative and a timeshare professional, and it's just not in the net result of their performance or pay check.

- Though you can't teach confidence, one can gain confidence.

- Being in control of one's life breeds confidence.

- A timeshare professional's confidence comes from their commitment of time, a laser focus on learning, dedication to understanding and the hard work of fine tuning.

- Confidence and the creation of a sale go hand in hand.

6. RELATIONSHIP – THE WARM UP

"A timeshare Professional's currency isn't money, it's their guest trust."

- T. A. Bragg

Would you ever marry someone without dating them first? Would you ever buy a home without walking through it? Would you ever buy a car without driving it? Most people would answer no to these questions. All three questions revolve around a long-term commitment. Guest don't buy vacations from you, they buy you.

From the second a salesperson meets their guests; a relationship begins to form. That relationship can be one of two kinds;

1. A relationship of trust
2. A relationship of distrust

A sale can only be made and kept if the guest-to- salesperson relationship is rooted in trust. As a relationship is developed, guests begin to open their lives to the salesperson, begin to open their hearts and the message begins to resonate with them, and begin to open their minds to the possibility of buying the product that day.

THE OPEN

The importance of opening these three components of your guests can't be understated. The more open guests are about their lives, the better you will be able to directly correlate their lives to your product. The more open minded they are, the more clearly they can see the many benefits of your product and how the product will better their lives. The more open the guests' hearts are, the more they are affected by the compelling emotional reasons to own your product. The salesperson with the high aptitude to build relationships quickly has a significantly better opportunity to experience timeshare sales success. For those who don't have that natural ability to cultivate relationships or the illusion of a relationship, they are forced to rely on tactics at their disposal to use during the sales process.

Obviously, as mentioned in previous chapters, a positive mental attitude and confidence from hello are critical. There are some specific things a salesperson must do at the point of hello. A salesperson must look each guest square in eye with a welcoming smile or expression on his or her face. Trust and the possibility of achieving a positive relationship are consummated at hello. The guests' impression of the salesperson is being formed immediately. While trust and the guest's impressions of the salespersons trust worthiness is most important, a guest's impression of how much the salesperson cares about them or if the salesperson only cares about himself or herself is also being formed. If a guest feels the salesperson doesn't care about them and their needs, there is no pathway to a sale. Trust cannot be built; it must be earned.

> Make them feel like they matter because they do.

Early on within the sales process, what are some ways a salesperson can increase trust and continue to build the relationship with their guest?

- Keep attention and focus on the guests, not yourself.
- Follow up on guests' answers; move past the surface of their lives with second and third level questions.
- Learn the reasons why your guest feel the way they do, have the opinions they have and want the things they desire, don't assume you know why.

The relationship the salesperson is building takes the duration of the entire presentation to solidify, but the foundation of that relationship is established in the first 30 minutes of the presentation. I believe the warm up is the most productive segment of a timeshare presentation in building that relationship. By definition, the warm up is the exploration and investigation of a guest's personal life. The warm up is also the guest's greatest opportunity to learn you care. A salesperson can't wait until the end of the sale to say, "Okay, now will you be my friend?" They have to like you, believe in you, and trust you within the first thirty minutes of the introduction or the sale will be lost.

THE BLESSING/CURSE OF GAB

When executing a productive warm up, a salesperson must avoid telling the guests about themselves. At this stage, the guest simply doesn't care about you yet, unless there is a direct correlation between the guest lives and the salesperson. For example, if the guest was in the armed services and so was the salesperson, it obviously makes sense to ingratiate the guest with that personal information. But if the guest states they're from Sacramento, they don't care that the salesperson is from Buffalo. It's never wise to initiate divulging your personal story to your guest. In fact, waiting for your guest to ask about your personal story is a tell-tell sign they have interest in buying your product. The guest wants to learn about who he's about to do business with. The more attention and interest a salesperson gives to their guest early in the sales process, the greater belief of the guest that the salesperson cares about them.

When asking personal questions of the guest, like "where are you from?" or "what do you do?" or "how many kids do you have?" a salesperson must follow up with a deeper level of questioning. These surface questions are called first level questions. A salesperson must go deeper or second level with their guest.

Example:

1st level "How many kids do you have?"

Answer: "We have two children."

2nd level "Are they boys or girls or one of each?"

3rd level "What are their ages?"

4th level "Do they play any sports?"

This is a very elementary scenario given, but it describes clearly how thorough all warm up and discovery questions need to be. This is showing genuine and specific interest in their lives. The more the guest divulges about their personal life the greater sense of a bond or relationship they feel they have with the salesperson. Like a psychiatrist, a salesperson wants to hear all their guest "business". Not asking follow up questions sends a signal to the guest that the salesperson is not truly interested in who they are. A person's actions will always speak louder than their words.

WHY?

I've found over my career, you never really understand someone until you know the "why" behind their actions. On the other side, if someone doesn't care to know the why, they probably don't care about the person. This isn't spoken, it's intuition. It's hard to trick intuition. Finding out a guest's "why" is a great tactic to trick intuition. Instead of a guest wondering if the salesperson really cares, when repeatedly asked their personal "whys," devolves a strong sense of someone listening to them and interested in hearing what they have to say. Everybody wants to be heard. This is a deep human desire. When the salesperson gives the guest his ear and gives the perception of "coming from the heart" by asking why, a strong relationship is quickly built.

As a timeshare salesperson, you have to dive deep into your guests' lives. The salesperson's actions of interest spark the birth of a relationship. Most importantly it creates a relationship of trust, which is going to be needed when asking for the business today.

Once a relationship is established and some level of trust has been built, a salesperson has now earned something important. They've earned the right to ask the tough questions. What do I mean by "tough questions?" The tough questions are questions that may be challenging to ask, like confidently asking for the sale today or asking for a justification of why not today. As the relationship gets stronger, not only does the salesperson earn the right to ask tough questions, but they also receive a greater level of honesty from the guest as well. When your guests become more honest with the salesperson, they also become more honest about the product being offered and the true benefits to themselves and their families. Simply put, being more honest with the salesperson inherently lets them become more receptive to the product. The trust developed when the relationship is built properly allows them to open-up. At the end of the day, that's all you need, the guest to be open to the idea of timeshare.

> "Know more than you say, think more than you speak & notice more than you realize."
> -T. A. Bragg

CHAPTER SUMMARY – RELATIONSHIP – THE WARM UP

- Guest don't buy vacations from you, they buy you.

- As a relationship is developed, guest begin to open their lives to the salesperson, they begin to open their minds to the possibility of buying their product that day and guest begin to open their hearts and the message begins to resonate with them.

- A sale can only be made and kept if the guest-to-salesperson relationship is rooted in trust.

- If guests feel the salesperson only cares about himself and doesn't care about them and their needs, there is no pathway to a sale.

- When your guest become more honest with the salesperson, they also become more honest about the product offered and the true benefits to themselves and their families

7. QUESTIONS

"Knowledge is having the right answer. Intelligence is asking the right questions. In Timeshare, you've got to have both."

-T. A. Bragg

One of the initial lessons taught on the first day of training class when entering the timeshare industry is that our guests retain only about 30% of what they hear. Years later I read that the brain is set up to engage questions, not statements. Which means when selling, if the salesperson is engaging the guest with statements rather than questions the brain of the guest is actually computing little of what it's being told and retaining even less. The verbal engagement has to be drastically greater than just "talking at" your guest to increase retention of the content in the presentation and comprehension of it. This higher level of engagement will translate to a greater impact of the value proposition of your product. The product sold in the timeshare industry is unique. No one walks thru the door "wanting" a timeshare. In fact, most couples make a promise to each other that no matter what, they're not buying anything. Sometimes, several hours later, those same people walk out smiling, giving hugs and saying thank you after spending

$15,000 or more. Timeshare is a unique product with a unique process. The timeshare product is considered by most to be a "big ticket" purchase. Most timeshare products are for a lifetime or at least several decades, so there's a very long commitment. Furthermore, this big ticket, long commitment product has to be sold same day. There are many challenges to overcome, and this is why this chapter is so important. A salesperson elevating the impact of their words inevitably gets more guests closer to the brink of buying their product. The more guests that are close, the more guests that are closed.

> "Listening to respond vs. listening to understand. Know the difference."
> - Unknown

THE ART OF QUESTIONING

There's a sales style I mastered as a sales representative and developed with sales representatives that worked under my leadership; it's called Question-based selling. I didn't invent question-based selling, but I did master it. I completely injected this style into my overall presentation and saw immediate results. Question based selling is deploying questions 80% of the presentation and making statements only 20% of the time. By using this strategy, the content of the presentation has more influence over guests. It forces the guests' brain to engage the words that are being spoken.

At first, the thought that 8 out of 10 verbal interactions need to be questions seems daunting. Some have even felt that it's impossible, but it's actually not that difficult. What one needs to first do is understand the difference between the two types of questions. A closed ended question and an opened ended question.

Closed Ended Question:

- A question that elicits a yes or no answer. Example- Are you traveling with your kids?

Open Ended Question:
- A question that elicits a multi word answer. Example- How do you feel about your accommodations?

Both question types are important but have two different functions. When deploying closed ended questions, it's important to say the question in a way that results in a "yes" response. It's critical to get "yeses" throughout your presentation. I've always coached representatives to ask at least 20 "yes questions" per presentation. This might seem excessive, but when a salesperson is asking questions 80% of the presentation, it's not excessive at all. The more a guest says yes during the salesman's presentation, the easier it will be to get a yes from your guest during the close.

In using the question-based selling method, many salespeople think to simply add more questions to go along with the many statements they already say during the presentation. The key is learning how to take your statements and turn them into questions. Closed ended questions are the easiest way to turn a statement into a question.

Example-
- The view here is absolutely gorgeous. vs.
- This view is gorgeous, wouldn't you agree?

Both are saying the same thing, but only one is ensuring engagement by the guest. The question has forced the guest's brain to comprehend the beauty of what the salesperson is showing them versus the salesperson's statement going in one ear of the guest and out the other.

Changing a statement into a question not only allows for greater guest engagement but also serves as small, incremental closes. These closes are called "tie-downs." The salesperson is tying down the positive affirmation of the guest to the feature or benefit the salesperson is presenting. Every time a salesperson receives a positive affirmation from the guest, it moves the guest closer to the BIG yes, the sale.

When a salesperson asks an open-ended question to the guest, the salesperson is eliciting an expressive response

Two things are important when asking open-ended questions:

1. Strategic Usage
2. Correct Word Usage

Opened ended questions are not meant to be used over and over again. The best usage is more strategic and tactful. Opened ended question are great for either following up a statement or when a salesperson makes a statement that is not converted into a question.

Example

- As an owner, every time you and your family get away, you'll stay in a spacious condo. How would that make you feel knowing your family will have so much space when getting away together?

Words have meaning and the meanings are important to understand. A salesperson can say something that appears to be just fine, but exchange one word and both questions have two different engagements.

Example

- What do you think about what I've shown you thus far? VS.
- How do you feel about everything I've shown you thus far?

Both questions are asking the same thing but elicit two different understandings.

Example #1: asking what the guest thinks gets the guest thinking, which can move the guest to needing to "think about it."

Example #2, is requesting the guest tap into their feelings and express how he "feels".

From a timeshare sales perspective, it's important we tap into our guests' emotional side of the brain, not their logical side. This is an emotional sale, and salespeople ask their guests to make an emotional choice to purchase same day. To overcome the challenges faced by salespeople on every tour, it's imperative the salesperson gets their guest in an emotional state of being to overcome those challenges. Guests rarely, if ever make a logical choice to spend $15,000 or more on a product that's has an extended commitment in just a few hours.

Opened ended questions are also another type of close. That close is called a trial close. A trial close is the ability of the salesperson to creatively get the guest to articulate positive feelings about the product or usage of the product being presented. It is important to seek out opportunities to trial close throughout the presentation.

When question-based selling, a salesperson must go 2nd and 3rd level, just like when asking investigative questions during the warm up and discovery. The difference is, instead of digging for more information, like during warm up and discovery, the salesperson is attempting to:

I. Obtain a greater commitment by the guest to the product or
II. Get the guest to verbalize the benefits of their usage of the product.

In other words, you want the guests to sell themselves. A salesperson wants their guests to state what could or should come out of the salesperson's mouth.

Example-

- Salesperson: This is a beautiful view. VS.
- Salesperson: How do you feel about this view?

Guest: This view is very beautiful.

Salesperson: Wouldn't it be nice to wake up to this view every morning when you come back on another getaway with your family?

Guest: Yes it would.

Salesperson: How would that make you feel, giving a view like this to your family?

    This is an example of making an obvious statement versus making the guest state the obvious and verbally acknowledge their positive affirmation of a feature of the product. The salesperson in the second example went deeper to secure a greater commitment to a feature of the product. These incremental commitments lend to a greater desire by the guest, to commit to owning the product same day.

While going 2nd, 3rd and 4th level is essential to consistent sales success, learning how to get the guests to sell themselves is powerful. The guest will always believe the words that come out of their mouths more than they believe the words that come out of the salesperson's mouth. Either the salesperson can say, "The view is beautiful" or the salesperson can creatively ask the question that leads the guest to say, "the view is beautiful." I call it "Self-Selling." Throughout the presentation, if the salesperson can get their guest to self-sell themselves eight or more times, most times a guest with the ingredients to own a timeshare product will say to themselves, "this is perfect for us" and move forward to buy the product. The salesperson put the guest in the position of selling themselves, literally. Get the guest to verbalize not just that is perfect for them, but why is perfect.

Why is the most powerful question available to a salesperson. It's the most open-ended and expressive question there is. Get your guests to not just give affirmation but explain their affirmation. By doing this, guests:

- Sell themselves
- Break their own pact
- Divulge more useful information that the salesperson can use when selling the product.

Why, is also great to ask after a blatantly obvious closing question.

Example:

Salesperson: Which accommodation would you prefer to stay in next time you and your family go on vacation, this condo or a hotel room?

The obvious answer is the condo. Questions like this can sometimes annoy your guest or even offend some. Asking why immediately after the guest responses with the clear cut choice or yes, turns the question from blatantly obvious, to the guest having to look within to articulate why it's important or better to them. Anything important to the guest is never stupid in their eyes.

Example:

Salesperson: Which accommodation would you prefer to be staying in next time you and your family go on vacation, this condo or a hotel room?

Guest: The condo

Salesperson: Why would you prefer the condo?

Their answer to the question is a newly discovered dominant buying motive for that specific feature or benefit that the salesperson can use during the sales process moving forward. The key is asking why strategically throughout your presentation, which greatly increases the amount of information that the guest gives the salesperson to analyze and then redeploy during the sales process. A salesperson asks whys in the warmup, asks whys in the discovery, asks whys when guests ask the salesperson questions about the program, and when they give an objection.

The mastering of why and how to deploy the question effectively and tactfully is a powerful tool in a salesperson's tool chest and will greatly improve their close percentage.

CHAPTER SUMMARY - QUESTIONS

- A salesperson elevating the impact of their words inevitably gets more guest closer to the brink of buying the product.

- When deploying closed ended questions, it's important to ask the question in a way that results in a "yes" response.

- Changing a statement into a question not only allows for greater guest engagement but also serves as small, incremental closes.

- A salesperson can say something that appears to be just fine, but exchange one word and both questions have two different engagements.

- While going 2nd, 3rd and 4th level is essential to consistent sales success, learning how to get guests to sell themselves is powerful.

8. VALUE PROPOSITION

"Sell what's important to your guest, not what's important to you."

- T. A. Bragg

How many salespeople take a close look at why a guest buys their timeshare product? How many have sought to diagnose and figure out precisely what triggered the guest's buying action? Being a sales leader for over 11 years of my career, I've had the opportunity to interact with tens of thousands of guests, closed thousands of deals and the wherewithal to study most of those encounters. What I found is, there are two constants:

1. Identified value by the salesperson
2. Recognized value by the guest

In other words, the salesperson found out what was important to the guest and attached that to the product. In essence, the salesperson helped the guest recognize what's important to them goes hand in hand with the product.

Because of this, you want to remove "yourself" when presenting to guest a sales opportunity. Yes, I know you must have targets and goals but that should not be the foremost thing on your mind. Keep your mind on what your guests' needs are and the benefits that are important them. Forget about your desires, your wishes and your targets.

Be service oriented, not target oriented. Keep your mind on what your guests' needs are and the benefits that are important them. Demonstrating value, presenting the benefits your guests need and developing trust should be the most important elements. When you make this your main focus, your instinct will work to figure out what problems your guests have and provide solutions to them. You are there to help your guests! As you master this, watch how your sales explode.

VALUE PROPOSITION

All guests have a set of core values. These core values are what's most important to them. Each timeshare company also has their individual core values, which embody what that company stands for. What most people don't realize is products have core values as well. How many timeshare salespeople have identified the universal core values of timeshare? Fortune 500 industries have, and the timeshare industry has as well. These core values are called the "Value Proposition" of the product. There are three core values of timeshare regardless of the type of timeshare (points or weeks) the type of ownership (deeded or not) or what the company is founded on. The three go as follows:

1. Family - Members spending quality time with the ones they love most, enjoying incredible experiences and creating lifelong memories together.

2. Forever/Lifelong - The ability to guarantee those special times for the rest of the members' lives, and in many cases for the rest of their children's lives and every generation after that.

3. Saving - Timeshare epitomizes the expression "more for less". Timeshare allows for members to give their families a better, more comfortable and functional accommodation for less money than a basic hotel room.

These impregnable values are undeniable to a guest with the necessary ingredients to purchase timeshare. Name a person who loves their family, but doesn't want to spend quality time with them. Name a person who wouldn't prefer to guarantee that quality time with the family they love. Name a person who doesn't want to give their family more while spending less money to do so. I haven't met a guest yet who claims to love their family most of all, sell me that renting hotel rooms for the family is better than giving their family better accommodations for less money. A guest can't sell me on that.

CORE VALUES

It's not enough to simply know the values of timeshare. A salesperson has to also find out the core values of their guest. Most salespeople attempt to identify their guest's core values during the warm up and discovery steps. The challenge with this idea is the salesperson is guessing or assuming through the guest's answers to traditional warm up and discovery questions. The salesperson is trying to decipher what the guest's values are instead of simply asking the guests. I found over my career that not just asking them, but also specifically having them write down their three core values led to more truthful answers. Now, once a salesperson is equipped with their guest core values, they can begin to present their product in terms that are directly aligned with the values of the guest. Presenting the product only in ways that are important to the guest and using the same language that's important to the guest is critical.

Example: Guest writes down "investing" as one of their core values. Salesperson would only talk about the financial benefits (rent vs own) of the product using same phraseology, i.e. "an investment in their family."

A salesperson must attempt to create those correlations and parallels between the guest's core values and the product's value proposition as many times as possible. By doing this, it gives the guest the intuition of the product being "perfect" for them.

There's a specific time and place in the presentation to have guests write their core values, in a way that will feel like fun and strengthen the relationship between them and the salesperson.

I've always coached the salespeople working under my leadership to use it as a transition from the warm-up to the discovery. To lessen the seriousness and bluntness of the question, I never coached the salespeople to ask their guest "what are your core values". Instead I coach them to ask "What are the 3 most important things to each of you at this stage of your lives?"

There are a few things that should transpire or get accomplished in this part of your presentation:

- Salesperson should have earned the right to ask a question like this because they have taken the time to establish a perceived relationship with the guest.
- Introducing the guest to picking up the pen and write when asked to, resulting in being more comfortable when asked later in the presentation to fill out credit application and/or agreement of terms to consummate the sale.
- Have the opportunity to identify the subtle differences between the couple. Couples are not monolithic entities and not identifying those differences many times are what separates both parties from no agreement to buy the product versus both parties agreeing to buy the product together the day of the presentation.
- Identify quick tell-tell signs derived from the guest's answers that are good and bad, but informative nonetheless. If a guest writes "being alone" as one of their core values,

it's a good chance the tour is going to be challenging and the salesperson will know to address that potential ensuing objection earlier in the presentation. If the guest writes "vacations, fun, leisure" or something of that nature, there's a great chance the salesperson has a great shot. We sell vacations, fun and leisure, right?
- The salesperson gets the opportunity to use not just their guest's words, but also their hand-written words to overcome the guest inevitable excuses that come up later in the presentation.

There must be awareness and understanding on the part of the salesperson as to why they're gathering this information and what to do with it once obtained. The information gathered should be deployed in conjunction with any and all features and benefits articulated to the guest throughout the sales process. If the salesperson talks about their product, it's stated along with something they learned was important to their guest.

As mentioned earlier in the chapter, this technique also allows for a seamless transition from warm up to discovery. After the guests have shared their values with the salesperson, they are obviously now in an information-giving mood. The salesperson should then have the guest write down three places each of them must visit in their lifetime which serves as a seamless transition into vacation discussions.

Though this seems like a basic exercise, there is much to gain by capturing three places (each) they must go.

I. It identifies specific destinations that a salesperson should solely focus on when showing properties that are available to them as members later in the presentation.
II. Allows for salesperson to paint mental pictures for the guest that is more heart felt. If showing the destination that hold great importance to the guest, seeing those properties will resonate and have a greater emotional impact.

III.   Salesperson can draw from those trips to describe usage or when presenting features of the product to the guest.

What I found is many sales people are using the incorrect verbiage when asking for these places from their guest. I hear constantly, "where is your dream vacation to?" The challenge with this question is the salesperson is asking for dreams. Dreams are hopes and wishes, they are not tangible enough in the guests' minds to base a presentation on.

I've always coached salespeople to enthusiastically ask "Where are 3 places each of you have to go before leaving this life. Where are 3 places you have to experience, no matter what?" I encourage salespeople to ask this question in a theatrical way because it emotionally prepares the guest to be excited, once they realize those destinations are tangible and real. The salesperson is able to infuse enthusiastic energy into the presentation, and that, along with the guests' excitement about visiting their desired destinations, increases their emotional "want" for the product. This exercise seamlessly transitions the salesperson into the succession of discovery questions.

As mentioned in the paragraph above, there is a certain level of theatrics or showmanship needed when using this information-gathering tactic. A salesperson must give their guests a show. They have to "sell it", because what's most important when deploying this exercise is getting as accurate and honest information as possible.

DBM

Obviously, it's also imperative for the salesperson to go 2nd, 3rd, and even 4th level with their follow up questions to the guests' written responses. This must be done wisely. There's only a certain allotted time per tour so every minute must be used in a way to maximize what the salesperson gets from the guests or what they're delivering to the guests. A salesperson cannot go 2nd level and deeper on every single answer. In fact, there's not a need to. Of the 3 answers of "what's most important" and "where they must go", usually 2 of the 3 answers are pretty standard. There's usually one that is unique; that's the answer you want to go 2nd and 3rd level with. That answer is the differentiating value and destination and will provide a greater understanding of each guest specific "uniqueness." That "special" answer is each guest's greatest dominant buying motive (DBM).

The concentration of the last three chapters has been on the mining of information from the guest. This detailed and deep-level information provides the salesperson with the necessary content to present the product, in a tailored, made to fit way, not in a generalized, one size fits all way. The product is the same, no matter which guest sits in front of the salesperson; what changes from guest to guest is the perspective the guests view the product through. Are they viewing the product through their eyes or through the salesperson's? A salesperson must position their presentation to be in exact alignment with the guests' needs, wants and desires. Being able to effectively do that is the difference between good and great in timeshare sales.

Lastly, by tying the guest values to the product's value proposition, the salesperson effectively boxes their guests into acknowledging the value of the product while insulating themselves from objections that they cannot overcome. The salesperson will be able to fall back on the product's three pillars:

1) Family

2) Forever/Life Long

3) Savings

To overcome false objections, "remind" the guest of their previous acknowledgments of their perceived value of the product, and reasons given by the guest during 2nd and 3rd level commitment questioning. Then remind them of what they stated in regards to how the product will benefit them.

Example:

Guest- *We like it, but need to think about it.*

Salesperson- *What would you specifically need to think about, guaranteeing quality time with your family forever or saving on the money that you spend to getaway to have quality time with your family? Remember earlier when you said...*

The objective is to pose a question that has an indefensible answer to the guest and address the contradiction made by the objection using the guest's own words. This makes the guest have to defend their previous statements before giving the salesperson additional objections. The salesperson reduces the number of maneuvers to the guest's planned strategy of saying no when they walked thru the door.

CHAPTER SUMMARY - VALUE PROPOSITION

- All of our guests have a set of core values. These core values are what's most important to them.

- Presenting the product only in ways that are important to the guest and using the same language that's important to the guest is critical.

- A salesperson must attempt to create those correlations and parallels between the guest's core values and the product's value proposition as many times as possible.

- There is a certain level of theatrics or showmanship needed when using this information gathering tactic.

- The product is the same, no matter which guest sits in front of the salesperson; what changes from guest to guest is the perspective through which the guest views the product.

9. LESS IS MORE

"The less you say, the less risk you run of saying something foolish,

even dangerous."

- Robert Greene

There's an old expression that goes something like this; "Just tell me what time it is, don't build me a clock." The meaning of this saying is simple, get to the point. So many times salespeople believe the more you say, the better. Or, the more you show the better. How about, the more you explain how it works the better? These statements are fallacies, but it's understandable why a salesperson could believe in the thought process. Why wouldn't giving more information about the programs be beneficial to the sale? Why wouldn't showing more of the product or its benefits, help get the sale? Have you ever heard the saying, "too much of anything can be bad for you?"

As timeshare sales people, we ask a lot of our guest. Our guest are asked to give up time on their vacation or their off time, to come spend two hours being sold a product they believe they don't want. The guest is then asked to comprehend and understand a product that many times is vast in its usage. Then the guest is asked to make an affirming choice to purchase and commit themselves long term to the product in just two hours. The fallacy lies in the belief that in presenting more of something the guest believes he doesn't want will somehow magically make him want it. That's like saying if someone went to a restaurant and ordered a meal that they did not like the taste of, getting a second helping and eating more of that same meal will make the patron somehow start to enjoy the taste of that meal. Is it fair to say that would not be the case? The same logic applies when selling timeshare.

> **THE RECIPE FOR SUCCESS**
>
> Add a dash of interest. Sprinkle a little bit of urgency. Mix with a splash of simplicity. Put a little bit of question-based selling. Finally, add a whole lot of value for them and viola you got a recipe for success.

At this time, in this day and age of timeshare or vacation ownership, the product is rarely as simple as a week of usage at a home property. Like everything in life, timeshare, the usage of timeshare and what timeshares can actually be used for, have evolved immensely over the decades. Remember, timeshares can now be used for not just accommodations, but airfare, cruises, car rentals, dinners, tours and dozens of other travel things. What timeshare has evolved into is a product that can fit anyone and be used universally, but the guests that come in to tour are not universal, they're specific. The guests are individuals that do not want generalities.

There's simply too much information to provide and still be digestible. When a person overeats, many times he or she gets a stomachache or becomes extremely lethargic. Neither reaction to overeating leads to action. A person who has overeaten is not jumping up and running a marathon. They say when someone is trying to lose weight, it's not about eliminating food, but about eating the right foods in the proper portions. The same philosophy applies when selling timeshare. In the sale of timeshare, the "right foods" are solely the interest, wants, needs, desires and values of the guest only. The salesperson must be disciplined enough to only present these things, not what's important to the salesperson and not everything the product can do.

Example #1:

Salesperson- Let me show this property I absolutely love. You'll love it too. It's in the beautiful Caribbean.

*** Note: Guest stated earlier in presentation, that they wish to not leave the US

Example #2: This product allows members to use it for cruising to. Let me show you how to use the product to cruise.

*** Note: Guest stated earlier they had a bad experience on their last cruise and don't believe they'll be going on any more cruises.

The quickest way for a salesperson to lead themselves down a path of "no sale" is to present, talk, show or demonstrate portions of the product, features or benefits that aren't directly in line with what the guests have already expressed as important to them. Showing guests a property or destination they have absolutely zero interest in visiting, or cruise options they'll never consider only moves the salesperson away from the sale and pushes the guest further from interest in the product, as well as disconnecting the guests from the parts of the product that do fit their needs. The salesperson has to serve the guests the "right foods" to get them to see enough value in the product to make a buying choice that day. The salesperson gets their shopping list for the "right foods" in warm up and discovery, using the strategies and tactics provided in the previous chapters.

HOW HOT DOGS ARE MADE

I'm not a huge baseball fan, I respect the game, but I grew up playing football and basketball. Although I don't love the game of baseball, there are few things better to me than going to a baseball game. The smell of the freshly cut grass, the lush gorgeous field, the sound of the crack of the bat when it connects perfectly with the ball, but most of all, enjoying a hot dog with all the fixings while watching the game. There's nothing like it. I love it. That made-to-perfection hot dog at games, just tastes so good, that. But has anyone ever told you how hot dogs are made? It's an interesting process to say the least. In fact, how hot dogs are made won't ever lend to the taste, flavor or experience of eating a hot dog. It will actually have the exact opposite effect. Knowing how hot dogs are made sometimes is so "interesting" that it dissuades people from wanting to ever eat a hot dog again. When selling a timeshare product, the salesperson doesn't have to tell the guest how the hot dog is made, they just have to get them excited on how great a hot dog tastes.

Many times, salespeople believe teaching their guest not just what the product will do for them, but how the product functions. This is a recipe for failure. Exposing the "how" will dilute the impact of the benefits of the product for the guest. The reason for this is simply because at that point, they don't care. Many salespeople are explaining the how before the guest even asked how. Remember, the guest doesn't care, until they ask. The "ask" is the indication that the guest cares specifically about that, and at that point only. When asked a question of usage by the guest, answer that question only. The question is not the opening or indicator that the guest wants to know everything about everything. It's an indicator that the guest wants to know a little more detail about what he just asked. In timeshare vernacular, this is referred to as "getting in the weeds."

Example:

Guest- *Can the points roll over?*

Salesperson- *Yes the points do roll over. Now the challenge is you can only roll them over during this time and that time. Also, you will only be able to use your points for this. There's a big fee to pay when you want to roll over your points.*

I am a firm believer in full disclosure. I also understand guests care about the additional information only after they've taken mental ownership. If a guest hasn't asked for the additional information, divulging it only moves the salesperson and the guests further away from consummating a sale. It's giving the guest too large of a portion for them to eat at that point which makes consumption of all the information challenging and the digestion very difficult. This results in the famous objection, "I need to think about it." Only give the guest the portions needed that gives the necessary calories (information) for action. Don't overfeed the guest.

THE WOULD AND THE WHY

The reality is, sometimes the salesperson doesn't even instigate the path of overselling, and they actually fall into a trap set by their guest. The trap is the guest asking question after question, but the answers to those questions are not a determinants or deciding factors to buy the product that day. It's information for information sake. To avoid stepping in this quicksand, don't answer the question with the answer; answer the question with another question. If the guest requests information for information sake, the salesperson must request the "would" and "why" of their questions before providing an answer.

Example:

Guest - *How many points does it take to stay in the four-bedroom?*

Salesperson - *Would the opportunity to travel with your family in a four bedroom be important to you?*

Guest- *Possibly.*

Salesperson - *Why would the opportunity to get away with your family in a four bedroom accommodation be important for you and your family?*

Now that the salesperson has pulled emotion out of the logical question asked, the salesperson can answer the original question. But now, the answer has relevance and positive impact because it's been filtered through emotional follow up questions first.

This goes back to the strategy of getting the guests speaking 80% of the time and the salesperson speaking only 20% of the time. If done in reverse, the salesperson telling the guest information for 80% of the time is not selling. Telling is not selling. Selling is asking smart questions, and engaging the guest's mind enough, they sell themselves.

THE PERFECT AMOUNT OF SELL

Finally, salespeople should never oversell the accommodations they provide to their guests before actually showing the accommodation. If the salesperson shows their guests a gorgeous 3-bedroom condo, it can be detrimental to describe the unit before they see it. Think of a movie everyone is talking about; everyone is raving about it. Finally, you go see the film and your expectations are through the roof because of all the hoopla. You watch with those raised expectations and most times, the film doesn't live up to your expectations. Not to say the film is bad, but you were expecting the best movie ever. The expectations actually stole some of the luster. The oversell is kryptonite to most sales representatives. The gift of gab can often turn into a double-edged sword and kill the very deal you spent numerous hours building upon. The sell is just like cooking chili, not too much of this, not too little of that, just the right amount of what's needed.

Let the unit sell itself. No matter what, it's better than a hotel room. Think back to the first time you saw the condo you're showing and how impressed you were? Your guest will most likely have that same reaction to the condo; you then build value from there. Don't minimize the impact of the visual beauty, space and utility of the accommodation. Let your guests' minds run wild then add their specific values to these impressions and reactions.

CHAPTER SUMMARY - LESS IS MORE

- As timeshare sales people, we ask a lot of our guest. Our guests are asked to give up time on their vacation or their off time, to come spend two hours being sold a product they believe they don't want.

- The quickest way for a salesperson to lead themselves down a path of "no sale" is to present, talk, show or demonstrate portions of the product, features or benefits that aren't directly in line with what the guests have already expressed that are important to them.

- If a guest hasn't asked for additional information, divulging it only moves the salesperson and guest further away from consummating a sale.

- Telling is not selling. Selling is asking smart questions and engaging the guests' mind enough, that they sell themselves.

10. WHERE ARE YOU? (TEMP CHECK)

"Everybody wants cake... but when given eggs, oil, butter, batter, a pan and an oven they get frustrated and leave the kitchen"

- King Sol

Being from Southern California, I grew up surrounded by several amusement parks. There's Disneyland, Knott's Berry Farm and Six Flags to name a few. I grew up going to these thrilling places all the time and developed a passion for roller coasters. At every amusement park, not just in Southern California, but nationwide, every park had a specific similarity. They all had big maps positioned all over the parks and all the maps share one distinct feature. The same phrase is used on every map at amusement parks. That phrase is "You are here" with some kind of icon. The question is, why does every map at an amusement park have the phrase "you are here?" Because, if you don't know where you're at, you won't know how to get to where you want to go. It's imperative that at multiple strategic points in the process, the salesperson must find out where their guests are in accordance to buying the product today. Without knowing this information is tantamount to walking in a barren desert, a thick jungle or an over grown forest without any instruments to help navigate.

THERMOMETER

In the timeshare industry, this concept of "where are you at" in the sell is called a "temperature check." Meaning, how warm and receptive are the guests to the product and buying it today. This must be gauged to determine which is the best and most efficient pathway to the destination of a sell? Without the salesperson knowing "where they are at", they might take the unnecessary long route or they may take the more difficult route, instead of taking the best route.

Guest will have one of three feelings towards the timeshare product being presented to them.

    I.   The guests LOVE the product
   II.   The guests like the product, but are not sold
  III.   The guests want nothing to do with the product

Is it fair to say, guests that have these three different feelings about the product are on completely different sections of the aforementioned proverbial map? If this is the case, would it also be safe to say, they have to take different pathways to get to the destination of the sell? This is why the temperature check is so important. It puts the "you are here" on the salesperson's map to better help navigate them to the sell. The path to get there for each one is vastly different.

ADHERING THE SPEED BUMPS

I am by no means advocating the salesperson changing up the presentation and process for every guest. Consistency in the presentation and process is a tenant of timeshare sales, but a salesperson must be able to adjust and alter their micro actions within the presentation and process to adapt to how the guest are feeling about the product.

If a guest "absolutely loves" the product, there's no need to oversell it; just get through the process quickly but thoroughly and present numbers. If the guest just "likes" the product, the salesperson needs to slow the process down and figure out their guest's concerns and questions. If the guest "wants nothing to do with" the product, the salesperson has to figure out why and be slightly more aggressive in presenting the direct correlations between what's important to the guest and the product, or simply identify a guest that the greatest value derived from the tour won't be financial, but the ability to work on a part of their presentation or process that needs improvement. Remember, the value to get from this Category C tour type is simply getting better by practicing or perfecting a specific skill set, strategy or tactic.

ADAPTATION

Think of these slight deviations as subtle as variations in a handshake. A man shakes another man's hand firmly and with intent, while a man will shake a child's hand lightly and with a kind touch. Both are handshakes, just applied slightly differently. The subtle adjustments timeshare professionals make in the midst of their standard presentation and process is what leads to more guest being closer to the sale at the time of closing. They find the best, fastest and most efficient path to the destination of a sale.

There are two specific points in a presentation where there's a fork in the road of the process, the salesperson is either going left or right. Going right represents getting to the finish line as quickly and as thoroughly as possible, and going left is slowing the process down and digging in. Rarely does the salesperson find himself traveling down the right side path, which is only 20%-30% of their presentations, but at least on those 20%-30%, the salesperson knows where they are and are much less likely to miss the sale. The two specific points in the process are:

I. Immediately after the group presentation is completed or after the salesperson has completed their product presentation
II. Immediately following final step before close

After the guest has had the opportunity to learn about the product in accordance and specifically tailored to their needs, a salesperson must figure out how the guest feels about the product and purchasing it today. There are many ways to go about this. Many times in the timeshare industry a famous close is given, "if this product is completely affordable to you and your family, is this something you want to own?" I personally am not a fan of this close, which acts as a "temperature check." I feel it is too broad and lacks any true commitments. Follow ups would be needed. Also, there's rarely any further information gained, such as what do the guest like or dislike about the program. Lastly, this question rarely comes with "today" attached to it.

Over the past decade, what I have encouraged the salespeople that I've led to do is to set up the temperature check, before checking for the guest's temperature with a series of questions. These questions allow the salesperson to get their guest into a positive state of mind, articulate to one another and to the salesperson their likes of the product and why those features or benefits are important to them. Once the salesperson has done those things, then they should ask the guest for their level of interest in owning the product that day, with the answer based on a numerical scale. All answers should come from all parties on tour ages 4 and above.

First Temperature check scripting:

Question #1

Salesperson: How do you feel about everything you've seen and heard so far?

Guest: (90% of the time guest will give a positive response It's nice, good, interesting, great, etc.).

- Question #1 is solely a "set-up" Question. The salesperson is literally setting up the guest to give a positive affirmation about the product. At this point, the salesperson should have shown only the parts of the program that are directly related to the guest wants, needs and values, so the guest should have nothing negative to say.

Question #2

> Salesperson: *GREAT! What jumped out about the product that grabbed your attention most?*
>
> Guest: *(Vast majority of the time, guest will give one of four answers)*

   I.   How nice the condos/properties are,
   II. How many places they can go,
   III. The flexibility of the program,
   IV. The ability to pass down to future generations- if applicable

- Question #2 is solely a tactic to conjure up positive thoughts that allow the guest to tap directly into the things they like most. The salesperson also has the guest verbalizing their individual likes that might not have been previously articulated out loud.

Question #3

Salesperson: Why would that be important to/for you and your family? How would that benefit you and your family?

Guest: (Articulates their why's)

- Question #3 is what I call the "self-sell" question. As described in previous chapter, "why" questions are the most powerful and self-deducing to the guest. The salesperson wants the guest to answer these questions from themselves and to themselves before going for the first hard close of "today."

Question #4

Salesperson: I get it! Or Very cool or Nice (Acknowledge the Guest Why's) I need you to put in perspective how you feel about the product, on a scale of 1-10. 1 you ABSOLUTELY hate the product to 10, you absolutely LOVE this product and want to own it TODAY. Where are each of you at, and folks, you CAN'T say 5. Where are each of you?

- Question #4 is getting a specific number that gives a more precise idea of what the next approach (path) is to get to the sale. This also allows the salesperson to differentiate and understand which guest interest is highest. The salesperson will need to better engage and work more on the guest with the lower interest.

Now the question is, what the numbers mean in correlation with the impeding strategy and tactics used. What numbers go with what path?

On-Site/Show Unit
- Numbers 8-10

These are guests who are in the "Ether". They want it, and it's up to the salesperson to not talk the guest out of purchasing it.

Go straight to some form of visual content, via "digital screen" of additional destinations or a wall tour to "paint pictures" for guest. If no wall or screen is available, go straight to the property.

- Numbers 6-7

6-7 traditionally indicates a high level of interest, but trust is in some way compromised. These guests should be sat down for a discussion on what specific questions or concerns they may have. Answer the guests' questions and address their concerns with some form of a "proof source". Many times, it's simply the guests' nature and not something the salesperson, site or company has done. The guest is just skeptical. This is why the "proof source" is so important.

- Numbers 1-4

A guest that has just a 1-4 level of interest has significant concerns that need to be addressed, acknowledged and attempted to overcome. The salesperson must demonstrate patience and peel back the many layers of the onion to get to the ROOT of their concern, fears, doubts or disbeliefs. There is zero to no trust in this perceived relationship and the exact time to fix it is at this time. The salesperson should not move on in their process until it's been established that the guest's interest is moving in the right direction or there is no way under any circumstances that the guest will open up to the possibility of owning the product. Sometimes a condition that prevents the guest from owning the product will present itself at this point in the presentation. The salesperson many times needs to "re-pitch" the product after they addressed the guest's concerns and possibly changed the perspective and narrative the guest initially had.

The 2nd temperature plays off the first temperature check and should take place immediately after the final step before "the close." The response to the temperature check is an indicator of if the guest is ready to transition into the closing process or not. Guests that are transitioned prematurely into the closing step before being "sold" will shut the door to the possibility of owning the product that day. A guest must be open enough that they're receptive to the possibility of owning the product same day.

2nd Temperature Check Scripting

Question #1

Salesperson: *Earlier, Mary, you said you were ___ and Bob, you said you were a ___. After seeing this product in its entirety, where are each of you now?*

Guest: *(Both parties provide answer)*

- Question #1 is to check how much the guest interest level has increased. The response to this question is normally an increase of 1 or 2 points. Sometimes, the number remains the same. Rarely, if ever, will the number decrease.

Question #2

Salesperson: *Great! What else do you need to know before being a 10 and my newest owner TODAY?*

Guest: *Price or how much does it cost? (99% of the time)*

- Question #2 thrust the presentation into the closing step of the process. The question is being asked, knowing the guest's response will be "the money". The question sets the guest up for the "final close" and reinforces TODAY.

Question # 3

Salesperson: *So what you're telling me is, if we can put a program together that fits PERFECTLY for your family, I'm looking at my newest owner? (Hand extended for a handshake)*

- Question # 3 is the final close. The salesperson is attempting to box the guest in and receive confirmation that they want to own the product today or flush out the final objection.
  Note: The hand extension is an extremely important action of question # 3.

THE PHYSICAL COMMITTMENT

The idea of a handshake is consummating a deal, so the physical attempt to consummate the deal applies added pressure to the closing question. That added pressure is called task tension. There must be a level of task tension during every presentation for a buying action to take place. Also, the handshake requires physical, not just verbal confirmation which lends to a much stronger commitment and less room for the guest to attempt to take steps back when the inevitable anxiety arises from the gravity of the action that is close to taking place… them saying yes.

When the salesperson sticks their hand out, 1 of 3 things will take place.

I. The guest will shake the salesperson's hand.

   This means the salesperson has a deal and should proceed through to the closing step.

II. The guest will initially extend their hand then retract their hand due to fear

   This means the guest has interest, but has more questions, needs greater understanding of a particular part of the program or is simply scared. What the partial gesture did indicate was that there is genuine interest subconsciously. The salesperson must take their time with this guest. Answer any additional questions and flush out any further objections or concerns. Slowly transition this guest into the closing step of the process.

III. The guest will decline the offer to "shake on it" and either put their hands in their pocket, behind the back or cross their arms. An objection will follow immediately afterwards

This guest is not ready to be closed. There are several more questions to be answered, indicating many times a lack of understanding or belief in what the salesperson has presented to them. This guest must be slowed down, re-pitched and more than likely needs a new face to take over the presentation or process, i.e. manager, closer or senior salesperson.

What the 2nd temperature check does is position the presentation to be closed or allows the salesperson to know that the guests aren't ready to be closed yet. The 2nd temperature check is like the navigational equipment pilots use to line the plane up with the runway for landing. The navigational equipment along with the many aeronautical statistics will tell the pilot if it's safe to land. The reactions and responses of the guest will tell the salesperson if it's safe to close their guest at that stage of the process.

THE TAKE OVER

An effective ally is the person who "takes over" your tour and closes it.

CHAPTER SUMMARY - WHERE ARE YOU? (TEMPERATURE CHECK)

- It's imperative that at multiple strategic points in the process, the salesperson finds out where their guests are in accordance to buying the product that day.

- Without the salesperson knowing "where they are," he might take the unnecessary long route, or the more difficult route instead of taking the best route.

- Consistency of presentation and process is a tenant of timeshare sales, but a salesperson must be able to adjust and alter their micro actions within the presentation and process to adapt to how they are feeling about the product.

- The handshake requires physical, not just verbal confirmation which lends to a much stronger commitment and less room for the guests to take steps back when the inevitable anxiety arises from the gravity of the action that is close to taking place - them saying 'yes.'

11. OBJECTIONS

"Timeshare Professionals don't hear the word "no." It translates to 'let me figure this out.'"

- T. A. Bragg

Fact #1 timeshare sales; every single guest booked to take a timeshare presentation is sitting in front of the salesperson solely because of the gift. Not one tour walks through the door with a credit card on their forehead, arms raised in the air, screaming I'm here to buy a timeshare. Not one guest is "interested" in learning more. With this being understood, there's one thing every salesperson can guarantee they will face, objections.

Most salespeople recoil at the sound of an objection. Most salespeople fear the objection. In actuality, objections are nothing to fear at all. In fact, objections are a salesperson's best friend in the selling process. What the Timeshare Professional knows is that there's no sale without the earlier presence of objections. The Timeshare Professional knows objections don't mean no, they actually just mean, not yet. Objections aren't real; they're a made-up excuse, veiled in very little truth.

The question to consider is, why do guests state and regurgitate objections? The answer simply is, the guests are not sold. The salesperson has not effectively correlated what's important to the guests with the features and benefits of the product, or the salesperson has not explained how the product will work for and benefit the guest. Most salespeople have no problem explaining how their product works, but very few know how to explain how the product will work for the guest in conjunction with how the product works. Salespeople must provide the explanation with the guests' lives, habit, needs and desires in mind. These two things must be done simultaneously. The guests' lives must be interwoven with how the product works. If this isn't done, it makes it more difficult for the guest to envision themselves using the product. Nothing can be generalized in the timeshare sales process. The site and company process has to be adapted to the guest in front of the salesperson.

Another important understanding is that objections are given at various stages of the process....

1. At the very beginning of the presentation.

Sometimes a guest comes in and within the first 5-10 minutes says to the salesperson, "you seem like a very nice person. I just want you to know, I'm not buying anything today." This proclamation is a sure sign the salesperson has a very good shot at deal. The guest will make this statement out of defensiveness. The guest went on a presentation before, were close to buying, but the pact was not broken well enough and the guest got out of the sales site without purchasing. The fact that they were so close to buying before, the guest's prepared strategy is to tell the salesperson immediately that they aren't buying with the intention of reducing the salesperson's efforts in trying to sell them. If the salesperson ignores the proclamation and gives a thorough and complete presentation, chances are high they'll get the deal.

2. A salesperson should be closing or asking the guest to buy their product relatively early and often throughout the sales process.

> Obviously, when a salesperson asks the guest to buy the product earlier on in the process, the guest has not seen the presentation in its entirety; they probably have not had all of their questions answered and are still learning how the product will benefit them. So naturally, the guest will come up with excuses on why not to buy the product. The guest aren't ready and don't have enough information to make an educated choice at that point. In fact, the point of the salesperson asking for the sale early is not to get a "yes," but to force out the inevitable ensuing objection early in the process, so that it can be isolated and overcome. Though the guest will more than likely say no in the early stages of the process, what asking for the sale does is move the guest closer to the sale. This is because the salesperson should have weakened, if not neutralized, the excuse and greatly minimized the belief in that excuse of the guest and its validity in why the guest should not own the product.

3. A salesperson can do an immaculate job executing the presentation, follow every step of the process, demonstrate tremendous value, cross every T and dot every I. They truly get the guest to genuinely love the product and yet still upon the final close the guest will retract, back pedal and give excuses of why not today.

> The guests love it, just not today. What the salesperson was unable to secure were any firm commitments throughout the presentation and process, which left the open the door for the guest to not commit to owning at the end of the presentation. These objections stem from two specific emotions;
>
> - Fear
> - Lack of Trust

In other words, the guests are either scared to say yes or do not trust the salesperson and the words they've spoken enough to make a buying choice that day.

What all of this means is objections that are given by guests have different meanings behind them, depending on when and what part of the process they are given. Understanding this prevents the salesperson from feeling defeated early in the process. This allows the salesperson to make the necessary adjustment during their presentation and allows for the salesperson to identify and isolate the guests feelings and concerns at the end of the process to address, disprove or overcome the excuses to finally get to the sale.

With the understanding objections aren't real, why guests give objections and at what stages of the presentation and process objections come, now we must look at what actions should take place once the salesperson receives an objection from the guest. The obvious answer would be to overcome the objection, and most times that would be the incorrect answer. Depending on the when the guests presents the objection, how passionate the guests are, how many objections are given at once and how many times the guests give the same objection are all factors into how the salesperson should react. Here are some of the ways a salesperson can react:

1. Meet the objection head on. - Example:

Guest- *I don't make same-day decisions.*

Salesperson- *Of course you do, you're a police officer. You make split decisions every day, don't you?*

2. Dismiss the objection. - Example:

Guest- *We might not go on vacation.*

Salesperson- *As you stated earlier, no matter what, you're going to get away and spend time as a family, right? So that wouldn't stop you from owning this today.*

3. Ignore objection. - Example:

Guest- *We don't like to fly.*

Salesperson- *So follow me and let me show you this.*

4. Agree with the objection. - Example:

Guest- *I don't know if this is for us.*

Salesperson- *I agree with you, if you're not got going to get away with your family and spend quality time together.*

5. Isolate the objection. - Example:

Guest- *We want to buy a house next year.*

Salesperson- *Ok, other than you wanting to buy a home next year, what else would stop you from owning this today?*

6. *Take away the product.* - Example:

Guest- *This commits us to having to go on vacations.*

Salesperson- *Hey, this might not be for you and your family. This is for families that do want to commit to getting away and spending time together.*

Like the old saying goes, "there are many ways to skin a cat." There're many ways for a salesperson to respond to objections. The timing of when the salesperson uses a particular way is key.

Early on in process/presentation use:

- Ignore
- Agree
- Take away

Middle of process/presentation use:

- Dismiss
- Isolate
- Take away

End of process/presentation use:

- Head on
- Isolate
- Take away

This is not to say this model is set in stone. We all know every tour is different, every guest is unique, but this is a conventional example for a typical tour.

One might notice the "Take away" falls in all three categories, suggesting it can be effective at any time in the presentation. This is correct. The "Take away" tactic is one of the most powerful tools available to salespeople. The take away does two things very well:

I. It disarms guest immediately. Guest are expecting the very opposite.
II. It plays on a very strong emotion - fear of loss. Emotion ignites action.

Some objections will require no further attention. Again, objections aren't real. Isolating, dismissing and agreeing with objections rarely need substantive action to overcome the objection. Using one of the three reactions above many times gets the point across and the salesperson can continue gathering information from, selling or closing the guest instead of get bogged down in a verbal tug of war over an excuse. But sometimes there are objections that must be overcome immediately.

Objections, perceived as real in a guest's mind, used as an impediment to own the product must be addressed and overcame. Avoiding these types of objections and/or allowing them to linger and resonate with the guest, only strengths the validity of the objection in the guest minds. In other words, excuses thought to be real by the guest, if unaddressed will become an insurmountable obstacle and won't be able to be overcame at the end of the presentation because it will be too late. Objections that are perceived to be real to the guest aren't overcome with a one-liner or magic pitch. These objections are overcome periodically during the presentation and the salesperson must sell to the objection making the objection the exact reason why the guest should own the product.

There are many tactics to overcoming objections. Let me share with you some that I've found to be very effective.....

1. Feel, Felt, Found

Example:

Salesperson- I "feel" exactly what you're talking about, in fact, I've had guest just like yourself that "felt" the same way, but what they "found" after joining is....

2. Third Party Stories

Example:

Salesperson- You know, you folks remind me of this great couple I gave a presentation to a little while back....

3. Sell to the Objection

Example:

Salesperson- That's exactly why you want to own this today....

4. Take Away and/or Give Back

Example:

Salesperson- This might not before you, but if _____ is important to you, then this might actually be perfect for you and you should keep an open mind.

FEEL, FELT, FOUND

Feel, Felt, Found is a technique used to overcome an objection using emotion, commonality and a first or third party story. When stating, as the salesperson, that they "feel" what the guest is saying, they are demonstrating empathy, which increases trust. By the salesperson aligning the guest's feelings with past guests who had those same feelings yet became owners, shows the guest they're not the only ones who felt the same way. It demonstrates that their situation is not unique, nor an impediment to ownership/membership. Lastly, the salesperson describes what past guests found by owning the product; this was the result. People love stories, and in timeshare, having the ability to be a creative, spontaneous and descriptive story teller is priceless.

THIRD-PARTY STORIES

Third party stories allow for the salesperson to passively overcome an objection. Again, people love stories and moreover, are willing to listen and hear with less bias, and better accept the message if delivered through a story. A third-party story is a story about a previous guest that addresses the fears, concerns or questions of the current guest. Telling smart, pinpointed, tactful stories is a very effective way to overcome an objection without offending or putting the guest in a defensive posture. This is usually a developed skill set that takes time to master.

SELLING TO THE OBJECTION

When a guest gives an objection, the guest believes it's a reason to not own the product. But there's a greater compelling argument for the exact opposite the salesperson should provide of the guest. This tactic requires very quick thinking on the feet. The salesperson is taking the objection and stating that as the reason to purchase, followed by a sound, reasonable justification for that perspective. The salesperson must have the belief system that every single household should own the product if it does not take food off their tables. If the salesperson truly believes this, then there's no excuse that the salesperson can't overcome using this technique.

THE TAKE AWAY

The take away is a powerful tool to bring the guest to the salesperson, rather than possibly alienating the guest and pushing him away. Sometimes guests come onto the sales floor ready for a battle. They're chomping at the bit to get in a verbal joust with the salesperson. Many salespeople believe immediately attacking an objection is coming from a position of strength. They feel it's strong, but rarely does a salesperson win the proverbial war by arguing with the guest. Winning the battle is not the objective. So, come from the exact opposite direction and catch the guest off guard.

Volcanoes erupt due to thickness of magma. If the magma becomes too thick, the gas bubbles won't escape and pressure rises. Don't lead the guest's temperament into eruption.

Using the take away tactic is passive aggressive by nature, giving the guest the feeling he's not being sold, while planting the seeds of loss of the product that provides exactly what's important to the guest. The key to the take away is giving it back. You have to give the product back to the guest in a way that proves the product consists of everything that's important to the guest and at the same time relevant to the objection. The give back might also be the follow up to the take away reaction.

The salesperson person reacts to the objection, depending on the type of objection, then follows up to overcome the objection. All objections are excuses, and all excuses need to be overcome.

Lastly, while 99% of objections are not real, there are a few objections that I recognize as being valid. These objections are actually conditions. If a guest has a condition that impedes them from owning the product, there is nothing the salesperson can do to obtain the sale that day. I feel there are only 3 true conditions:

I. Middle of escrow
II. No credit
III. No cash down payment

These are the only true barriers to a sale from my perspective other than extreme ignorance. Salespeople want to avoid getting tied up in the weeds, arguing the guest excuses. Simply react, overcome and move forward.

CHAPTER SUMMARY – OBJECTIONS

- Every single guest booked to take a timeshare presentation is sitting in front of the salesperson solely because of the gift.

- Objections are a salesperson's best friend in the selling process.

- The "Take Away" tactic is one of the most powerful tools available to salespeople.

- Feel, Felt, Found is a technique used to overcome an objection using emotion, commonality and a first or third party story.

- A third-party story is a story about a previous guest that addresses the fears, concerns or questions of the current guest.

- If a guest has a condition that impedes them from owning the product, there is nothing the salesperson can do to obtain the sell that day.

12. HOPE & WISH

"The distance between dreams and reality is called action."

– Ben Francia

Everyday there are thousands of timeshare salespeople that wake up hoping for a deal, wishing for a "lay down" while expecting success. The timeshare sales industry is as competitive, challenging and as difficult as any sales industry in the world. This is why the industry can be so financially rewarding. What most salespeople fail to realize is the sacrifice, dedication and commitment necessary to achieve those rewards. The individual timeshare salespeople that are consistently performing at a high level have put in the work and completely understand their guest's choice to purchase after two hours of being in their presence had absolutely nothing to do with luck. In this industry, lay downs come few and far between. More often than not, you will succumb to more challenging to near impossible tours. That's why the Timeshare Professional is keen on the ability to create the deal to advance themselves to the next level of success.

THE TOOL BELT

Success in timeshare sales is a coming together of honed skill, supreme confidence, laser focus, a raging competitive spirit and belief in one's self. Your skills are the tools in your tool belt that creates the deal. The Timeshare Professional makes sure that they have all the necessary tools to get the job done without revealing all the tools in their arsenal. Each tour requires a different set of tools in closing the deal. A Timeshare Professional knows there are no good tours or bad tours; they're only shots and no shots. They believe if there's any type of shot, they have the right tools to get the job done.

> The tools needed to build a table are wood, screws, a ruler, a saw and a hammer. There's no need to bring a jack hammer, or a forklift. Supply yourself with the right tools for every situation. Leave the others.

STEPS TO THE DEAL

Deals do not manifest themselves and the guests don't somehow just figure it out. The environment for a sale is created. That creation is done through smart questioning, deep fact finding, artful and descriptive storytelling. Combined with a talented explanation which takes a guest that's against owning the product to strongly considering the product.

The next step in the evolution of a sale is making the deal. Timeshare professionals make deals by simply asking for the sale without fear or hesitation. Timeshare professionals are comfortable navigating the inevitable impediments they will face. They refuse to see these challenges as impassable but see them only as small obstacles. Every time the salesperson asks for the sale, the guest gives an excuse which moves the guest closer to the deal. By being confronted with the possibility of owning the product, justified by the guests' own words, makes the idea of owning the product possible. This is when sales are made.

Finally, comes the moment in every presentation when the deal has to be taken. Guests don't jump across the table, grab the pen out of the salesperson's hand and ask where do they sign up. Getting the guest to want the product is far different from getting the guest to want the product enough to buy it that day. There're powers that are measured by the guest, but are not tangible, like trust, understanding and perspective that suspend the guest in a state that has them vulnerable and susceptible to being closed. The guests don't know why they love the product, but they do know they do love it. What the guests do know is, they like their sales person, they trust them believe them and want to do business with them. At this point the Timeshare Professional instinctively knows to seize the sale. The guest will not make that choice for the salesperson or themselves, the salesperson must apply and bring forth the right amount of pressure to trigger buying action.

    The point of this chapter is to emphasize the fact that the salesperson holds his fate in his own hands. There's no magic, mysticism, hoping or wishing involved in the art and science of timeshare sales. It's only skill, preparation and competence. When the salesperson controls his destiny, his chances of winning are predestined. The question every salesperson should ask himself or herself while looking in a mirror is, "Who are you?" Even beyond that, ask yourself "Have you done more than enough? Do you believe?" If the answer is yes, to anyone of those questions, then the desired result will follow. Professionals look to themselves to accept responsibility and hold themselves accountable; they never place blame.

CHAPTER SUMMARY - HOPE & WISH

- The sales professional makes the deal by simply asking for the sale without fear or hesitation.

- The timeshare sales industry is as competitive, challenging and difficult as any sales industry in the world.

- The Timeshare Professional makes sure that they have all the necessary tools to make sure they can get the job done without revealing all the tools in their arsenal.

- Guest don't jump across the table, grab the pen out of the salesperson's hand and ask where do they sign up.

- The salesperson holds his fate in his own hands.

13. HARD WORK & DEDICATION

"The moment when you want to quit, is the exact moment you've got to keep pushing."

- T. A. Bragg

During my time leading a team in New York City, I experienced a unique culture that in all my years in the industry I experienced only once before. Throughout the sales floor I felt a different type of energy that permeated every square inch of each room. The energy emitted from this floor took me back to my early days of being a sales representative, in Las Vegas, and made me realize the key intangibles that were needed for me to be successful. A leader on the floor established the sites war cry, a mantra, that resonated in me from the second I heard it. Leadership says: HARD WORK and the sales floor screams: DEDICATION.

   I.   Hard Work
   II. Dedication

To obtain success in the timeshare industry, the timeshare professional's career needs to be built upon these two conditions. My dedication of constant improvement, sharpening my tools, attacking my weaknesses, and to outperform everyone else became the bread and butter of my ascension.

Dedication, when applied vigorously, emulates obsession. This obsession was a key component to my mastery of the art and science of timeshare sales. Dedication nor hard work can exist without the other. If a sales representative wants to be dedicated to mastering his skill set in this industry, he has to be hard working. It's a self-taught, inner willed ambition that drives one to their desired level of success.

By no means is this job easy. This industry is one of the most challenging professions you will ever experience, but it's also one of the most rewarding. You sell a product that after your guest say yes, they sign paperwork, go home with a few books and a heart full of dreams of any trip in the world being possible, yet nothing tangible to back those dreams up. At the end of the day, we don't sell vacations, we don't even sell dreams, we inspire them.

You will learn in this business that in order to seek the riches you deserve, you without a doubt have, to be dedicated mentally and physically.

Motivational speaker Dr. Eric Thomas once said, "Luck is for leprechauns." There is no wishing in this business. No amount of hope will ever bring an ounce of luckiness. It frankly comes down to the individuals who become so skillful, so hard working, that no matter what impediments arise, success is always the outcome.

When we are discussing the work one must put in to become successful in this business, we aren't just talking about reading books. We aren't talking about going to trainings or role-playing third party stories either. The type of work in this business that you have to put in is the brutally honest self-analysis. The Timeshare Professional reflects on their last tour from beginning, to the end, dissecting what they did great and what could they have improved on. The professional is assessing why their guest didn't buy or why they did, always seeking either perfection or mastery - perfection of their delivery and mastery of their tools. This only comes through hard work and dedication. It's recognizing the pattern in which guests transform their doubts into positive beliefs. Self-analysis brings you that much closer to closing the gap between good and great. You have to organize your thought processes into various scenarios on how you could've approached the situations set forth and what you can do to improve next time.

When you come to the realization that we are artists simply using our words to create life inspiring illustrations for our guests, one becomes aware of the importance of fine tuning their wordsmithing and how essential it is to their craft. It's the most impressive tool the salesperson can develop. The dance between you and the guest must be coordinated in such a way that every step taken is intentional and every word spoken is calculated. You, the lead, must guide your guest into every question already knowing what the answer will be. That also means foreseeing the objections before they come to pass.

> "Lack of direction, not lack of time, is the problem. We all have twenty-four hour days."
>
> -Zig Ziglar

The salesperson who's dedicated to becoming a Timeshare Professional and seeks to achieve this level of mastery will undoubtedly commit themselves through this arduous process until they have attained this high level of abilities. These are the individuals that generate the greatest number of new owner sales, write the most volume and receive the highest incomes month in and month out. After a while, it becomes a numbers game to the best in the business. You give the Timeshare Professional 30 tours and they will out-perform month in and month out, consistently and efficiently. Performance at this level will earn the rewards their specific company has to offer from expensive dinners, lavish trips, bigger bonuses and all the extra honors that come with SUCCESS.

CHAPTER SUMMARY - HARD WORK & DEDICATION

- Dedication, when applied vigorously, emulates obsession. This obsession is a major key component to mastering this game that we play each and every day.

- There is no wishing in this business. No amount of hoping and wishing will ever bring an ounce of luckiness.

- The Timeshare Professional that seeks to achieve top-level mastery of hard work and dedication will dedicate their selves to perfecting it until they too have achieved that mastery level.

- Highlighting the benefits and features of the product that pertain to the guests lives, is absolutely vital.

14. URGENCY

"You only have 120 minutes. Don't delay. Don't second guess. Don't doubt. When the opportunity presents itself, close. When the impulse is there, close. When the intuitive nudge from within is there, close. That's your job, and that's all you have to do."

- *T. A. Bragg*

It's almost as if the moment comes unexpectedly. One moment you're waiting in the lounge, munching on a snack, talking to coworkers, discussing VPG and bonus levels you want to hit, then boom! The first wave starts and from here on out, the time you so lavishly had, begins to slip away from you. You must know that in this industry, time is of the essence and is never on your side.

If you're lucky, you'll get 120 minutes with your guests to transform those hellos into congratulations. It's so critical that you immediately get your guests into that buying mood because every second wasted only widens the gap for making a sale. It's imperative that you move with a sense of urgency.

The Timeshare Professional who moves with a sense of urgency understands that the challenge is too big to waste a moment. There's only so much time you can waste before you've completely lost the deal. Ether is not only triggered from a sense of urgency, it is sustained throughout the tour by it as well. To move, walk and talk with a sense of urgency, you can't be thinking about what to say or what to do. You have to internalize the fundamentals described in this book that allow you to just perform. The clear and defined fundamentals must be proactively executed throughout the presentation, and proactivity always allows for sustained urgency.

The guest is on the defensive, attempting to explain the unexplainable; not buying your product and to give their families the best out of life and saving money doing it. This is why in the previous chapter we discussed the importance of internalizing your pitch, which allows you to modify accordingly when time becomes too valuable to lose. Your tone in your pitch will become the most tactful move for you, especially as the clock ticks away. You can literally adapt your pitch to exactly what the guests need to hear. But, this will never be executed well if urgency has not been developed throughout the flow of your pitch. You are allotted 120 minutes to get to the "yes". When you create urgency it will, without fail, carry your guests across the finish line and get your guests to the promise land. When continuously incorporating urgency into your pitch, it will allow you time to pivot between different talking points that move your guests in the direction of becoming your newest owner.

BACK OF THE PACK

Urgency is not only important to close the sale at work, it is also extremely important for yourself and your career. A Timeshare Professional understands, there's no next month or next year; there's only today. Timeshare is simply a today business, and to not possess the personal urgency to push yourself to success will lead to stagnation, mediocrity and falling to the back of the pack. Talent can only take a salesperson so far; it truly is the fire in one's belly and the voracity for success that gets him to the top.

Urgency becomes the internal clock of a Timeshare Professional's career. Every month, every sales board across the industry is wiped clean and everyone is back to zero again.

Suddenly, there's no differentiation between the seasoned vets and the fresh-faced rookies. The playing field is even and the wheel is balanced. I can't emphasize enough that during this time, the Timeshare Professional takes advantage of this opportunity to stride ahead of the rest of the pack. The urgency kicks in along with the realization of how they start the month, will propel them to a strong finish and positioned to finish at top-level.

> Knowing is not enough; we must apply. Being willing is not enough; we must do.
> - Leonardo da Vinci

When you inflame your urgency at the start of every month, pressure eases off your shoulders, and instead of panicking towards the end of the month, you can dominate it.

URGENT WHEN NEED BE

Now some of you might already have that sense of urgency. For you go-getters that were simply born with the "go," I ask that you fine-tune your urgency. Be urgent to the things that matter, like the little things. Be early every day - not just on time, be positive, be available, want every opportunity, want to train and get better. These all take effort and effort is what fuels urgency. Urgency shouldn't be a constant motion. It has to catalyze when it's needed. Otherwise, patience becomes hindered in the process. Urgency and patience must coexist, but often clash with each other.

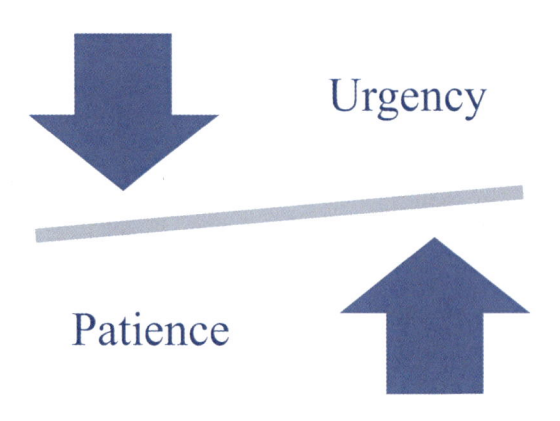

Urgency

Patience

The more urgent you are, the less patient you become. The more patient you are, the less urgent you become. It's a constant seesaw between the two, but when balanced correctly, will produce top-level results.

You don't want to be so urgent that you scare your guests. Strategically place urgency in certain aspects of your presentation to motivate your guests to act and produce the outcome you DESIRE.

CHAPTER SUMMARY - URGENCY

- If you're lucky, you'll get 120 minutes with your guests to transform those hellos into congratulations.

- The Timeshare Professional who moves with a sense of urgency realizes the challenge is too big to waste a moment of time.

- When continuously incorporating urgency into your pitch, it will allow you time to pivot between different talking points that move your guests in the direction of becoming your newest owner.

- The more patient you are, the less urgent you become. It's a constant between the two, but when balanced correctly, will produce top-level results.

CONCLUSION

In order to prevent lulls in the site's production, I instituted a fun referendum for my salespeople. They were encouraged to take a trip every three months to any of our resorts, and comeback with pictures and stories. Not only did this increase their sales by 20%, they were refocused and dialed in on why we sell the best product in the world.

The purpose of this book is to:

- Identify the core fundamentals and necessities which every frontline salesperson needs to understand, perfect, then master
- Equip every frontline timeshare salesperson with the insight, perspective, new belief system and tools to face the challenges of this profession.
- Narrow down the key strategies and tactics to get the average guest closer to the yes

Success in the business is not a sprint, nor is it a marathon. What success is in this industry is exactly what you put into it and what you want it to be. Especially when you realize and appreciate the opportunity that lies in front of you. How long will it take fortify your 90%? How greatly will your confidence grow? When will you identify your motivation? When will you stop hoping and quit wishing? How hard are you willing to work? How dedicated are you willing to be? How much urgency do you have in your belly? With every skill taught in this book, how long will it take you to master them? The answer is clear in that we hold all the answers deep inside. We have the ability to simply make the choice to be great or not. It's all on us, and that is what I love about this business. This book is the exact definition of what a representative can become if he or she applies the principles laid out in these chapters.

This book is not to train you; it's to inform and develop you. There is a significant difference between the two. Training is telling; developing is explaining the "why." A key of mastery is the understanding of the why. When you understand the why you strip away all the limits to what you, as the salesperson, can create and develop into. The sky becomes your limit and the ceiling has disappeared. With a new recalibrated perception on how you look at the selling process as a whole, the goals you target can be accomplished because you now know the hows and whys on accomplishing them. When you apply the principles of this book every day, you will see improvements in leaps and bounds. Application is the key to it all.

The hard work and dedication needed for this career is not easy. If after reading this book in its entirety you feel less prepared than before, this business is probably not for you. My intention was not to sugar coat what it takes to be great in this industry. Timeshare professionals aren't sugar coaters. If anything, timeshare professionals are the most realistic, straightforward individuals in the sales profession. Time is more valuable than money in this industry, leaving timeshare professionals no choice but to dismiss nonsensical hurdles while directing all of their focus to practices that will produce the best results. You cannot be a faint-hearted individual in timeshare. Your inner strength has to be stronger than the challenges faced every day on every tour.

The most powerful point in this developmental guide is creating an opportunity for you to see clearly your strengths as well as weaknesses from each chapter you study, and build up and strengthen your inner core to become mentally stronger in this business.

Implementing the keys of this book into your daily development is the first step to becoming a Timeshare Professional.

Always remember to:

- Assess daily
- Strengthen your 90%
- Know your motivation
- Role-play question-based selling to ensure retention in the guests
- Exude confidence
- Embrace objections as opportunities
- Execute every opportunity available
- Work with heightened urgency
- WIN, WIN, WIN, AND WIN.

Allow yourself time to grow in this business. Make sure you travel as much as you promote it to your guests. Go see the different resorts your company has to offer. Bask in the opportunity of what your guests can truly attain. Remember, we don't sell timeshare; we sell fun. Learn and then teach others what you know; there's enough pie for everyone. Perform these tasks and you will see yourself transform from a sales rep to a Timeshare Professional.

Made in the USA
Monee, IL
30 October 2022